Reading
Globally, K–8

WITHDRAWN

We dedicate this book to our grandchildren—Avelea, Benjamin, Aubrey, Lauren, AJ—and all the children of their generation who will be our future global citizens.

Barbara A. Lehman   Evelyn B. Freeman   Patricia L. Scharer

Reading
Globally, K–8

Connecting Students to the World
Through Literature

CORWIN
A SAGE Company

KH

 Corwin
A SAGE Company
2455 Teller Road
Thousand Oaks, California 91320
(800) 233-9936
Fax: (800) 417-2466
www.corwin.com

SAGE Ltd.
1 Oliver's Yard
55 City Road
London EC1Y 1SP
United Kingdom

SAGE India Pvt. Ltd.
B 1/I 1 Mohan Cooperative
Industrial Area
Mathura Road, New Delhi 110 044
India

SAGE Asia-Pacific Pte. Ltd.
33 Pekin Street #02-01
Far East Square
Singapore 048763

Printed in the United States of America

Library of Congress Cataloging-in-Publication Data

Lehman, Barbara A.
Reading globally, K-8 : connecting students to the world through literature / Barbara A. Lehman, Evelyn B. Freeman, Patricia L. Scharer.
    p. cm.
Includes bibliographical references and index.
ISBN 978-1-4129-7392-2 (paper w/cd)
    1. Literature—Study and teaching (Elementary) 2. Children—Books and reading. 3. Multicultural education—United States. I Freeman, Evelyn B. (Evelyn Blossom), 1948- II. Scharer, Patricia L. III. Title.

LB1575.L37 2010
372.64—dc22   2010029363

This book is printed on acid-free paper.

10 11 12 13 14 10 9 8 7 6 5 4 3 2 1

Acquisitions Editor:	Carol Chambers Collins
Associate Editor:	Megan Bedell
Editorial Assistant:	Sarah Bartlett
Production Editor:	Amy Schroller
Copy Editor:	Adam Dunham
Typesetter:	C&M Digitals (P) Ltd.
Proofreader:	Ellen Howard
Indexer:	Judy Hunt
Cover Designer:	Karine Hovsepian

9/2/11

Contents

List of Figures

Acknowledgments

This book has been a labor of love for two reasons: It reflects our passion for children's literature and international perspectives, and it provided a welcome opportunity (increasingly rare these days) for the three of us to collaborate as authors. However, in neither case could we have accomplished it by ourselves, and there are many to whom we owe our gratitude and thanks.

Regarding our collaboration, we want to thank the teachers who contributed teaching vignettes for this volume. Their pieces add important descriptions that bring first-hand classroom experience to the ideas we suggest. We also recognize our graduate students at Ohio State University who researched and wrote profiles that enrich the information about international authors behind many of the books we cite. The names of these contributors appear with the pieces they wrote throughout this text. We are deeply grateful for the valuable assistance provided by doctoral student Lisa Patrick with editorial tasks and to both her and another doctoral student, Denise Davila, for the thoughtful, detailed feedback they provided for early drafts of selected chapters. We hope you are all glad to have been a part of this venture.

With respect to our international perspective, we have greatly benefited from working with our colleagues in IBBY and USBBY, who have broadened our horizons and from whom we have learned so much about children's literature around the globe. One of us, in particular, recognizes professional friends in South Africa, who have so generously shared their insights and justified pride in their own literature. To all of these individuals we owe so much, and we hope that we have honored your work with this book.

To our excellent partners at Corwin—Carol Collins, our editor; Megan Bedell, associate editor; Sarah Bartlett, editorial assistant for permissions; Amy Schroller, production editor; and Adam Dunham, copy editor—we are indebted for your vision, patience, wise advice, astute feedback, attention to detail, and unwavering encouragement. We also thank the reviewers who read and responded to a draft of this book in manuscript form and whose names and affiliations are listed below. Your comments were a great help in our revisions. We hope everyone is proud of the result.

Finally, as always, to our spouses—Dan, Harvey, and John—your love and support throughout the long process has meant everything. We hope you think the journey was worth it!

Publisher's Acknowledgments

Corwin gratefully acknowledges the contributions of the following reviewers:

Joan Irwin, Professional Learning Consultant
Newark, DE

Carol Gallegos, Literacy Coach
Hanford Elementary School
Hanford, CA

Kay Kuenzl-Stenerson, Literacy Coach
Merrill Middle School
Oshkosh, WI

Vicki Seeger, Instructional Coach
Pleasant Hill Elementary School
Topeka, KS

About the Authors

Barbara A. Lehman, EdD, is Professor of Teaching and Learning at The Ohio State University, where she teaches graduate courses in children's literature and literacy at the Mansfield Campus. Her scholarly interests focus on multicultural and global children's literature and child-centered literary criticism. She coedited *Teaching With Children's Books: Paths to Literature-Based Instruction* (National Council of Teachers of English [NCTE], 1995) and coauthored with Evelyn Freeman *Global Perspectives in Children's Literature* (Allyn & Bacon, 2001). Her third title, *Children's Literature and Learning: Literary Study Across the Curriculum*, was published by Teachers College Press (2007). She has had articles published in *ChLA Quarterly, Children's Literature in Education,* and the *Journal of Children's Literature,* among others. She has coedited the *Journal of Children's Literature* (Children's Literature Assembly of NCTE) and *Bookbird: A Journal of International Children's Literature* for the International Board on Books for Young People. She has served on and chaired book and author award committees, such as NCTE's Award for Excellence in Poetry for Children Committee, the Children's Literature Assembly's Notable Books in the Language Arts Committee, the Hans Christian Andersen Award U.S. nominating committee, the USBBY's Astrid Lindgren Memorial Award nominating committee, the International Reading Association's Arbuthnot Award Committee and the Notable Books for a Global Society Committee, and the ChLA Article Award Committee. She is president-elect of USBBY (to be president in 2011). She was a Fulbright Scholar in South Africa during 2004 and 2005 and the 2009 recipient of the Arbuthnot Award from the International Reading Association.

Evelyn B. Freeman, PhD, is Dean and Director of The Ohio State University–Mansfield. She also serves as Executive Dean for Ohio State's regional campuses. Dr. Freeman is professor in the School of Teaching and Learning and teaches courses in children's literature and language arts. Her research interests focus on multicultural and global children's literature and nonfiction literature for children. She has served as coeditor of the *Journal of Children's Literature, Bookbird: A Journal of International Children's Literature,* and the Children's Books column of *The Reading Teacher.* She has coauthored three books: *Using Nonfiction Trade Books in the Elementary Classroom* (NCTE, 1992), *Connecting Informational Children's Books With Content Area Learning* (Allyn & Bacon, 1997), and *Global Perspectives in Children's Literature* (Allyn & Bacon, 2001). Dr. Freeman has written numerous book chapters and her articles have appeared in *Language Arts, Bookbird,* and *The Reading Teacher.* She has presented at professional conferences nationally and internationally. Active in professional organizations, Dr. Freeman chaired the Notable Books for a Global Society Committee and the Orbis Pictus Award for Outstanding Nonfiction for Children Committee. She has served on USBBY's Astrid Lindgren Memorial Award Nominating Committee. In 2007, she received the Distinguished Service Award from the National Council of Teachers of English. Dr. Freeman is immediate past-president of the Children's Literature Assembly of NCTE.

Patricia L. Scharer, PhD, is a professor of education at The Ohio State University and Reading Recovery University Trainer. Her research interests include early literacy development, phonics and word study, and the role of children's literature to foster both literary development and literacy achievement. Her research has been published in *Reading Research Quarterly, Research in the Teaching of English, Educational Leadership, Language Arts, The Reading Teacher, Reading Research and Instruction* and the yearbooks of the National Reading Conference and the College Reading Association.

She has served as coeditor of the *Journal of Children's Literature, Bookbird: A Journal of International Children's Literature,* and the Children's Books column of *The Reading Teacher.* Professor Scharer is also coeditor of *Extending Our Reach: Teaching for Comprehension in Reading, Grades K–2* (Literacy Collaborative at The Ohio State University, 2001) and *Guiding K–3 Writers to Independence: The New Essentials* (Literacy Collaborative at The Ohio State University, 2007). She is coauthor of *Rethinking Phonics: Making the Best Teaching Decisions* (Heinemann, 2001). She is a member of the national Literacy Collaborative Trademark Committee and recently conducted federally funded research in partnership with University of Chicago, Lesley University, and Stanford University.

Introduction

When Alice Rumphius (in *Miss Rumphius* by Barbara Cooney, 1982) was a little girl, she listened to her grandfather's "stories of faraway places" and declared that "When I grow up, I too will go to faraway places, and when I grow old, I too will live beside the sea." Her grandfather replied, "That is all very well, little Alice . . . but there is a third thing you must do . . . . You must do something to make the world more beautiful."

In today's world, those "faraway places" aren't so far away any more and may not seem as exotic as they did to Miss Rumphius. Many of today's children will visit the faraway places of other lands in their lifetimes. Yet, many others won't, although their lives will be greatly affected by what happens in distant countries whose people and cultures may still seem utterly foreign. Indeed, the classmates sitting next to them in school may be recent immigrants from faraway places. Thus, the need to understand the experiences and perspectives of these recent arrivals and places from which they come is immediate.

In the past 40 years, the United States has made remarkable strides in raising awareness of and appreciation for the multiple cultures and ethnicities within our own country (even while, admittedly, much work remains to be done to achieve true equity and justice). Can we say the same thing about our accomplishments toward international understanding and respect? At a time when our nation often seems preoccupied with terrorism from abroad and securing our national borders from perceived threats—political, economic, religious—perhaps we need to remember Alice's grandfather's lesson that we all "need to do something to make the *world* more beautiful" (emphasis added).

What can that be? Young Alice did not know, but she eventually discovered what she could do, and that became her legacy. We, too, can do something to make the world more beautiful by bringing the world home to our children through literature. Then, if they grow up to be world travelers, they will feel like they already know something about the faraway places they visit; and if not, they will have their horizons widened far beyond the places they experience first hand. Either way, they will have the opportunity to enrich their lives through the knowledge about and empathy for other people they can gain in the pages of well-written children's books.

In the aftermath of World War II, Jella Lepman, a German Jew and founder of the International Youth Library and the International Board on Books for Young People, had a vision of the capacity of children's books to build bridges of understanding between children across cultures and countries (Lepman, 1964/2002). She labored unceasingly to make her dream a reality so that another war like that one would never happen again. More than ever in our contemporary world, we need to fulfill that promise. As teachers, we *can* bring the world to our students in a positive manner with the help of excellent global literature. We can inspire the next generation to reach out and welcome diversity, to eagerly learn more about other people, to work for solutions to global challenges with fellow human beings from around the world, to promote world peace, understanding, and cooperation rather than strife and conflict.

Does this appeal sound high-minded and idealistic? We hope so! We also believe that it is realistic, possible, and necessary. It is vitally important, and it can be *our* legacy. This book aims to convince elementary and middle school teachers of the importance and relevance of embracing a global perspective, to demonstrate the value of global children's literature for gaining that viewpoint, to introduce global literature available in the United States, to inspire you to incorporate this literature in your instruction across the curriculum, and to provide practical ideas for doing so.

Organization of the Book

This book is organized into two major parts preceded by an opening chapter. The first chapter provides a background of the context in which American children's lives are affected by an increasingly diverse society within our country and by the world beyond our national boundaries, an overview of global children's literature past and present, and how we define *global literature*. We also demonstrate the need for global literature in our multicultural society: specifically, ways that this literature benefits *all* children's cognitive, emotional, moral, and social development. We explain how the use of global literature in the elementary and middle school curriculum can help to accomplish this goal.

Part I, then, focuses on ways to infuse global literature throughout the curriculum. We first describe a framework for literary theme studies and how these can be a means for integrating the curriculum. From this foundation, we explore the purposes and uses of global literature in specific curricular areas, including language arts; the content areas of social studies, science, and math; and the arts. In each curricular area, we include practical teaching ideas and book examples from all genres and highlight many award-winning titles.

Part II addresses several issues that you are likely to face as you try to include more global literature in your classroom instruction. We explain how we can determine the authenticity of global books. We also discuss other factors in book selection, such as literary merit and how translation influences a book's quality, and we address such contemporary pressures teachers face as standards, mandated curricula, testing, and local community attitudes. In the final chapter, we explore next steps for teachers, including ways to get started with using global literature in your teaching.

Throughout the book, you will find some special features. These include profiles of authors, illustrators, and other prominent figures in global children's literature. We also provide classroom vignettes written by teachers who already use global literature in their classrooms. Ideas for technology connections and suggested children's books appear in each chapter. A particularly important feature of this book is the companion CD with three resources: (A) a list of further reading for your own personal and professional development, (B) resources that can help you locate and continue learning more about global literature, and (C) annotations and interest levels of all the children's books cited in this book. Be sure to check this final resource regularly as you encounter books mentioned that appeal to you.

Our overall goal is for this book to be both an inspirational and practical guide for building intercultural bridges with global children's literature across the curriculum. Let's follow the example of Miss Rumphius. Let's make the world more beautiful by bringing it to our students. We invite you to join us on a global journey through the wider world of children's literature.

1

The Need for Global Literature

Gardening and cooking: These topics often bring pleasure, as most of us love food, and virtually every culture has its delectable specialties. Many people enjoy and take pride in raising their own produce; for some, it is a necessity. The late 1990s saw the publication of four children's books that used these motifs to demonstrate and celebrate the diversity of our society. In Erika Tamar's (1996) *Garden of Happiness,* the Lower East Side of New York City becomes the setting of a community garden for Puerto Rican, African American, Indian, Polish, Kansan, and Mexican neighbors. In *Seedfolks,* by Paul Fleischman (1997), a Cleveland, Ohio, neighborhood garden brings together 13 strangers from Vietnamese, Rumanian, white Kentuckian, Guatemalan, African American, Jewish, Haitian, Korean, British, Mexican, and Indian backgrounds. *Mama Provi and the Pot of Rice,* by Sylvia Rosa-Casanova (1997), portrays how a Puerto Rican grandmother's pot of *arroz con pollo* transforms into a multicultural feast with the help of white, Italian, black, and Chinese neighbors in one city apartment building. Another urban dwelling forms the setting in Judy Cox's (1998) *Now We Can Have a Wedding!* when Jewish, Japanese, Chinese, Italian, and Russian neighbors contribute to a multicultural banquet for a Greek-Mexican wedding.

Cities in the United States often are the places where small communities encompass such diverse cultures, so perhaps it is unsurprising that these four books use similar premises. In addition, according to U.S. Census ACS demographic estimates for 2006 to 2008, the whole nation is becoming rapidly more diverse, with whites comprising about 74% of the population, Hispanics/Latinos (of all races) 15%, African Americans 12%, Asian Americans 4%, Native Americans 1%, and mixed race 2%. (Because of rounding and the inclusion of Hispanics/Latinos in multiple categories, the percentages total more than 100%. See U.S. Census Bureau, n.d.) Most noteworthy, the Hispanic/Latino population is growing at the fastest rate, followed by growth among Asian Americans and mixed ethnicities. These numbers also highlight at least two trends: the speedy increase in racial diversity as whites drop to the lowest growth rate and the rise of mixed-race individuals. Moreover, as reported by *Newsweek* ("Stirring the Pot," 2009), by 2050, the white proportion of the population likely will decline to 47% of the total, and the Hispanic/Latino population will rise to 29%. Clearly, our society is indeed evolving multiculturally.

We also are becoming more global, with an estimated 12.5% of the population in 2006 to 2008 being foreign-born, a segment that has grown by nearly 6.6 million since 2000. Compared to 1900 when 86% of immigrants arrived from Europe, in 2007, 53% were Latin American and just 13% were European ("Stirring the Pot," 2009). In addition, we are growing more diverse linguistically. According to 2006 to 2008 census estimates, nearly 20% of the population age 5 and older, speak a non-English home language, and of these, 62% speak Spanish at home. Indo-European (everything from French to Russian and Hindi) and Asian/Pacific Island (Chinese to Tagalog) languages rank distant third and fourth places, respectively, after English and Spanish (U.S. Census Bureau, n.d.).

Likewise, although statistics are unknown regarding how many Americans travel or live abroad each year, many do or have done so, which is likely becoming more common in an age of globalization. As noted by Bartholet and Stone (2009), "For the generation of Americans coming of age now, some of the most significant opportunities—for work, investment, recreation and learning—will be global" (p. 52). In addition to actual travel, there is growing use of the Internet for social networking and other real-time exchanges from around the world. Thus, the demographics show a context in which the need for global perspectives is increasingly compelling and ever more relevant in children's lives.

The Importance of Global Literature in Children's Lives

Arizona Houston Hughes (the protagonist in *My Great-Aunt Arizona*, by Gloria Houston, 1992) taught her students not only to read words and figure with numbers but also "about the faraway places they would visit someday," even if only in their minds. She understood the importance of a global perspective in education, and as an avid reader, she also would have recognized the power of books to bring the world to the most remote places, such as her small village in the Blue Ridge Mountains.

Children develop rapidly in every way throughout the elementary grades, and, according to Evans (1987), these students "are not only developmentally ready but . . . [the elementary years] might be an especially important age to include global concepts in the curriculum" (p. 548). To understand why, let's consider how international literature can benefit four aspects of child development: cognitive, emotional, moral, and social.

Cognitive Development

When little Alice (in *Miss Rumphius*, by Barbara Cooney, 1982) declared that she would visit faraway places when she grew up, she displayed a child's natural curiosity and need to learn. Global books can help to satisfy those needs and prepare children for the places they will go. They can learn about the world, its people, and their lives, histories, cultures, hopes, dreams, and challenges. These stories stimulate children's imaginations and broaden their horizons, as the exemplary teacher, Sister Anne (in Marybeth Lorbiecki's, 1998, *Sister Anne's Hands*), knew when she took her second graders "to the library to visit islands in the ocean and countries across the sea." Through reading, children can learn to recognize similarities and differences between themselves and children in other nations and develop critical thinking as they analyze these comparisons. Such learning and skill development generates cognitive growth.

Emotional Development

Beyond engaging the intellect, global books also elicit emotions. As children learn about others' lives and make comparisons to their own, they can develop empathy for other people and appreciation for differences. Many young children everywhere can identify with

Jamela's predicament (in *Jamela's Dress,* by Niki Daly, 1999) when her imagination overcomes her sense of responsibility as she envisions herself a queen wrapped in Mama's new dress fabric and parades down the street. Even with a setting in a predominantly black township in South Africa, this is a familiar story of play and its feelings of delight and wonder. However, such total immersion in the fantasy of the moment also can sometimes generate feelings of dismay, regret, and even loneliness, and offer catharsis to readers who have experienced similar emotions. All these emotions will not seem "foreign" to most American children. Jamela could easily be friends with Max (in Maurice Sendak's, 1963, *Where the Wild Things Are*), and most youngsters can empathize with both characters. Empathy, an essential element of emotional development, enables children to identify with and share the feelings of others. For instance, in *From Another World*, by Hans Christian Andersen Award-recipient Ana Maria Machado (2005), set in contemporary Brazil, Mariano and his friends experience empathy for a slave's ghost as they solve a mystery and learn some history about their country. Readers, in turn, will empathize with the characters in this book. Through reading global literature, children can develop emotionally in positive ways.

Moral Development

Cognitive and emotional development also pave the way for moral development. Elementary children are developing their sense of right and wrong. They may be ready to consider moral dilemmas that extend their sense of fairness beyond their own self-interests (Kohlberg, 1976). Global books offer rich opportunities for young readers to vicariously experience ethical problems and explore issues of justice and equity. Even children who have never experienced segregation or being made to feel shame about their skin color may be outraged by the cruelty and injustice in Dianne Case's (1995) *92 Queens Road* when young Kathy is ordered to leave an apartheid-era whites-only beach in 1960s South Africa because of her ethnicity. They can make historical connections between Kathy's experiences and Cassie Logan's in the segregated American South of the 1930s (in *Roll of Thunder, Hear My Cry,* by Mildred D. Taylor, 1976) or the little girl who is forbidden from drinking at the "whites only" water fountain in a segregated Mississippi town (in *White Socks Only,* by Evelyn Coleman, 1996). Through reading and discussing these books, young readers can grow in their moral reasoning.

Social Development

Finally, children also develop socially as they learn to take multiple perspectives. This can happen through both reading—different books on the same topic or themes, for example—and discussing global books. In one such book, *Samir and Yonatan,* by Daniella Carmi (2000), readers witness two different perspectives when a Palestinian and an Israeli boy become friends in a hospital. They also can hear their classmates' different interpretations, especially if they include children from Arab or Jewish backgrounds. Teachers will need to establish an atmosphere of trust and respect in the classroom for this kind of exchange to be positive, however. (See *Building Character Through Multicultural Literature: A Guide for Middle School Readers,* by Rosann Jweid and Margaret Rizzo, 2004, for a discussion guide of this book.) As Hazel Rochman (1993) asserted, "Books can make a difference in dispelling prejudice and building community . . . with enthralling stories that make us imagine the lives of others" (p. 19). Such literary experiences can widen children's sense of community to encompass the world, and global literature can play a vital role in children's social lives.

The Contemporary Context

In addition to the importance of global literature already discussed in this chapter, there are other reasons for instilling a global perspective in children. We live in a global community, in which the peoples of the world are becoming increasingly interdependent. The everyday lives of children are no longer limited to traditional national borders. Global communications provide instant news and information about wars and conflict, natural disasters, famous personalities, sporting events, and all aspects of life. Lawmakers, as well as educators, have recognized the need to educate U.S. students for global citizenry. In his 2009 State of the State address, Ohio's Governor, Ted Strickland, indicated that as part of his P–12 school reform package the curriculum should "add new topics including global awareness" (para. 98). The state of Wisconsin has formed a statewide International Education Council, and Idaho has created a task force that focuses on ways to enhance global awareness. What reasons are precipitating the current emphasis on global awareness? Why is it important for children to possess the knowledge, skills, and attitudes to become successful global citizens? The many reasons regarding this need can be clustered into several areas: economic, environmental, world health, national security, and international immigration. In the following sections, we explain each area and present a brief example of how international children's literature relates to it.

Economic Reasons

In his international best seller, *The World Is Flat,* Thomas Friedman (2007) discusses the forces that have created a more level playing field for all countries in terms of equalizing economic opportunity. Friedman identifies 10 forces that have flattened the world and points out that multinational companies, outsourcing, and the advancing technologies have changed the way we view world economics. In the United States, the amount of money spent on importing goods has now exceeded the amount of revenue received from exporting goods. Although the United States is certainly among the strongest economies in the world, recent world events have necessitated a critical look at our economy and its relation to others in the world. In addition, the vast number of people throughout the world who live in poverty is a great concern. Many young children in various parts of the world must work to help support their families, sometimes forgoing their own education. For elementary children, these economic reasons relate to social studies concepts like goods and services, the world of work, and careers. Ted Lewin's (2006) book *How Much? Visiting Markets Around the World* transports readers to Thailand, India, Peru, Egypt, and New Jersey. Through text and colorful, detailed illustrations, children can compare and contrast these outdoor markets as people buy and sell their wares.

Environmental Reasons

In recent years, attention increasingly focuses on environmental issues and how we can sustain our planet earth. These concerns affect all countries and peoples around the globe. Many topics are included in this area, such as biodiversity and endangered species, climate change, global warming, energy sources, natural disasters, conservation, and pollution. Children need to gain knowledge about this area as they become the next generation to seek ways to solve these challenges. Children are interested in the rainforest, endangered animals, conservation efforts, and going green. Teachers can share international books that provide diverse perspectives on these subjects and describe worldwide efforts to address these concerns. Teachers can introduce students to international conservation efforts by sharing *Quest for the Tree Kangaroo: An Expedition to the Cloud Forest of New Guinea* (2006). Author

Sy Montgomery teamed with biologist and photographer Dr. Nic Bishop to present this fascinating account of the expedition, illustrated with color photographs. The book's final section, "Conservation at Home and Around the World," suggests what young readers can do.

World Health

The 2009 H1N1 flu scare certainly raised attention to world health and how disease can spread quickly from one country to another. A host of world health issues exist, such as infant mortality, hunger, HIV/AIDS, other infectious diseases, and safe drinking water. The United Nations has established eight specific goals to achieve by 2015 including several in the area of health: reducing child mortality, improving maternal health, and combating HIV/AIDS, malaria, and other diseases (World Health Organization, 2010). The United Nations observes World Health Day on April 7. Children can easily relate to this universal concern about health as they experience illness themselves and deal with health issues of parents, grandparents, and others close to them. For instance, nine-year-old Kati in Thailand copes with her mother's serious illness, amyotrophic lateral sclerosis (known as ALS or Lou Gehrig's disease) in the translated book, *The Happiness of Kati*, by Jane Vejjajiva (2006). This book will prompt much discussion among children.

National Security

The terrorist attacks of September 11, 2001, radically changed the way Americans think about national security and have led to many new laws and public policies. In addition, children are bombarded with televised news about war and conflict around the world, some of which involve the United States directly. Books can help children to gain insight into countries that are engaged in war and relate to children living in lands experiencing conflict. Tony O'Brien and Mike Sullivan (2008) traveled to Afghanistan to interview children who, like their U.S. peers, desire peace and education. In their photoessay, *Afghan Dreams: Young Voices of Afghanistan*, Nadira, age 11, who lives in Kabul, describes how she has "been working on the carpets for six years. Because of the work I don't go to school" (p. 42). Tajalaa, age 8, lives "on the peak of a mountain with my mother and one small brother. There is no electricity. We live with a lamp and carry our water up on our backs" (p. 53). Young readers can begin to understand how living in a war-torn country affects the daily lives of children like themselves.

Children need to recognize the human consequences of war and how many innocent people are negatively affected. For instance,

Alia Muhammad Baker, the Chief Librarian of Al Bashra, Iraq's Central Library, became a true heroine when she rescued the library's books in 2003 at the start of the Iraq war. Children can learn her story in *The Librarian of Basra: A True Story from Iraq*, an informational picture book by Jeanette Winter (2004).

Figure 1.1	Classroom Vignette: Lives in Hiding: Identification Through Character and Point of View (Grades 6–8)

I wanted students in my language arts class to examine their attitudes about human rights, prejudice, and responsibility to others while learning literary elements, such as characterization and point of view, as they read *The Upstairs Room*, by Johanna Reiss (1972), and *The Diary of Anne Frank*, dramatized by Frances Goodrich and Albert Hackett (1956).

The students initially worked in groups to complete a K-W-L (know, want to know, learned) chart on the Holocaust, followed by a whole-class discussion to share their charts and thoughts about the issues. Finally, the students were told to imagine this scenario: "The government issued a statement saying you and your family, because of your religious faith, will be deported to another country to help rebuild their war damage, and they promise it will only be temporary and then you will be allowed to return home after the war. Additionally, the government issued a warning that anyone caught attempting to escape or hide will be put to death." Students silently lined up on the side of the classroom that represented what they would do: escape and hide or do what the government told them to do, for fear of being punished. A debate then ensued regarding the students' choices, with some students changing sides after hearing their peers' opinions.

Next, books were distributed to the students who had chosen the "escape-and-hide" side of the classroom, as I explained to them that they were like the main characters in our books because they went into hiding. After a book talk introducing each book and including some of the information from the groups' K-W-L charts, the students from this side of the classroom received their books.

Writings from students confirmed that these texts encouraged them to identify with the narrators' perspectives. For example, Ben wrote about point of view: "Without Anne's diary and Annie living to write her story later, I wouldn't have been as interested in hearing about what they lived through, but because they were really telling their own stories, it made me want to keep reading. I should write about my life for generations to come. It would not be really my story if my mom or dad wrote about my life. No one knows what's really in my mind but me, even though we all live in the same house."

Many students commented on how brave and inspiring the characters were. Wanqui wrote, "Both main characters have positive attitudes throughout the texts. They try to make the best out of their situation, even though they are living in terrible conditions. I've had challenges in my life and it's like Anne and Annie let me know that even though my case wasn't as bad as theirs, I should try to be positive and think of the future too." Darin wrote, "Although they were young, they made a difference in our world. Anne Frank died, but she is still an author and also a teacher sharing her life experience with us. Annie lived and went on to write a book of her experiences. Without these books, we would not have known how kids our age were affected by actions of others." Thus, comparing and contrasting the main characters in the two texts allowed my students to understand that people are all the same, yet different, and that we may have different coping mechanisms.

Teacher: Angela R. Thomas, NBCT, Grades 6–8 language arts, Attica, Ohio

International Immigration

The United States is truly a nation of immigrants, and increasing numbers of students attend school whose native language is not English and whose cultures differ from the mainstream culture of the United States. Some children have come to the United States by choice; yet others are refugees fleeing terror and persecution. Immigration policy has been debated by state and federal legislators and has become a controversial topic in the United States. Books can provide children insights into the thoughts and feelings of immigrants. The award winning children's author and illustrator Peter Sís (2007), who defected to the United States as an adult, reflects on his childhood in Czechoslovakia in *The Wall: Growing Up Behind the Iron Curtain*. In the British book, *Making it Home: Real-Life Stories From Children Forced to Flee*, compiled by Beverley Naidoo (2004), children from Kosovo, Bosnia, Afghanistan, Iraq, Congo, Liberia, Sudan, and Burundi tell their own stories of forced migration and life as a refugee in new countries, like the United States.

Our world is shrinking, and today's children will become adults in a truly global community. Children's books can support their understanding of the world and help them develop a global perspective. The next section of this chapter provides background and context for the current status of global children's literature and the availability of these books in the United States.

History and Availability of Global Children's Literature

According to Publishing Central (2009), 29,438 children's books were published in the United States in 2008. Of these, some originated in other countries. Exactly how many is difficult to determine, but they represent only a small percentage (less than 5%) of the total number of books. Although all genres of children's books are distributed in the United States and translated into English, picture books, classics, and folk literature dominate the market. For example, on the 2008 New York Times 10 Best Illustrated Books list, three are international. The author/illustrator of *Ghosts in the House* (Kohara, 2008) lives in London. Canadian publisher Groundwood publishes two of the books: *Skim* (Tamaki, 2008) and *The Black Book of Colors* (Cottin, 2008), a translated book originally published in Spain.

Many of our beloved children's classics like *Heidi* by Johanna Spyri (1880/2002), *The Adventures of Pinocchio* by Carlo Collodi (1881/1988), and *Pippi Longstocking* by Astrid Lindgren (1945) are all translated books. In fact *Pippi Longstocking,* first published in Sweden in 1945, is an example of the enduring popularity of classics. Florence Lamborn translated the book into English, and Viking published it in the United States in 1950. Since then, the book has been issued in paperback, packaged in boxed sets with other books about Pippi's adventures, and made into a DVD. There is even a Pippi Longstocking doll and costume. In 2007, Viking released a new translation by Tina Nunnally of this beloved book.

Figure 1.2	Profile: Astrid Lindgren

The passionate, famous Swedish writer, Astrid Lindgren, made an impact worldwide with her amusing children's books. Born as Astrid Anna Emila Ericsson in Vimmerby, Sweden, on November 14, 1907, Lindgren grew up on a farm with parents who encouraged her to read literature every day and develop a creative imagination. This freedom and encouragement guided her toward a career as an editor at Raben & Sjorgren from 1946 to 1970 and as a world-renowned author of such classics as *Pippi Longstocking* (1945), *The Brothers Lionheart* (1973), and *The Children of Noisy Village* (1947). Lindgren is recognized as the foremost Swedish contributor to modern children's fantasy, according to *The Encyclopedia of Fantasy* (Clute & Grant, 1997). During her time as editor, Astrid Lindgren also inspired and influenced the translation of the world's best-known books for Swedish children.

On the writing side of Lindgren's career, her stories, especially the ones about Pippi Longstocking, have been introduced to the world through reprints in over 90 languages. Loved by children from around the world, Lindgren would receive 150 letters a week from her young fans, to most of which she would then respond personally. Pippi Longstocking, named by Lindgren's daughter, has become an icon for independent and spunky girls. As a nine-year-old girl living on her own, Pippi inspires readers to search inside themselves and find the courage to do and be whatever they want. Some adults may criticize the lack of parental control in the tales of Pippi as outlandish and unrealistic, but Lindgren wanted children to be seen as human beings without being oppressed. Just being "loved" was Lindgren's foundation for good behavior in children.

As a warm, independent role model, Lindgren was known for her humanitarianism and activism for children's rights. She felt it was important for her books to portray loving relationships, freedom, and empowerment for generations of children. In 1994, based on this philosophy of life, Astrid Lindgren received The Right Livelihood Award, given by The Right Livelihood Award Foundation, designated for outstanding vision and work on behalf of our planet and its people. This prestigious prize has become widely viewed as the "Alternative Nobel Prize." Among the other awards this author received in her lifetime were the Hans Christian Andersen Award (1958) for her contribution to children's literature, the NILS Holgersson Plaque (1950), the Swedish Academy's Gold Medal (1971), and the German "Friedenspreis des Deutschen Buchhandels" (1978). The Astrid Lindgren Memorial Award, described in Resource B on the companion CD, is named in her honor. Astrid Lindgren died on January 28, 2002 at the age of 94.

—*Julie McWhorter*

Other classics, such as *The Secret Garden,* by Frances Hodgson Burnett (1911/1988); *The Tale of Peter Rabbit,* by Beatrix Potter (1902); and *Winnie-the-Pooh,* by A. A. Milne (1926), were first published in England before gaining popularity in the United States. Some of the earliest recipients of the coveted Newbery Medal were set in foreign countries. In 1925, *Tales from Silver Lands,* by Charles J. Finger (1924), received the medal for a collection of 19 folktales retold by the author who learned of them when he traveled in Central and South America. The *Trumpeter of Krakow,* by Eric Kelly (1928), the 1929 Newbery recipient, is historical fiction with the setting of the 1462 Kraków, Poland, fire. The 1933 Newbery, *Young Fu of the Upper Yangtze,* by Elizabeth Foreman Lewis (1932), recounts the story of Fu Yuin-Fah, a Chinese boy who dreams of becoming a coppersmith. So, attention to global books is not new to children's literature in the United States.

However, before these classics came folklore—the oldest oral stories of humankind and sometimes described as the root of all literature. These tales include Aesop's fables; Greek, Roman, and Norse myths; Mother Goose nursery rhymes; King Arthur legends; and ballads and folksongs. Some of the most well-known tellers of folktales have written in languages other than English: Charles Perrault (French) and the Brothers Grimm (German). Thus, English versions of these beloved stories all necessitated translation. Beyond these familiar examples, though, all world cultures have their own traditional literature, handed down from generation to generation, from creation myths, pourquoi tales, trickster and noodlehead stories, and hero and tall tales, to variants of well-known folktales, such as Cinderella. Folktales from diverse international cultures are prevalent in the United States, some first published in the United States and others imported from their countries of origin. Comparing the motifs and themes across this collective body of world literature reveals the commonalities and distinctiveness of each culture's literary heritage.

Fantasy novels first published in other countries are also readily accessible in the United States. Simon Boughton (2006) of Roaring Brook Press points out that: "It's no accident that fantasy fiction—from C. S. Lewis to Philip Pullman to J. K. Rowling to Garth Nix—is internationally popular; in creating their own worlds, they have a universal setting. And successful fantasy deals with large universal themes" (p. 17).

Nonfiction books from other countries have also become more available with increased attention to that genre in the United States. London-based Dorling Kindersley (DK) now publishes its nonfiction titles in 51 languages. These extensively illustrated books feature innovative, appealing formats and cover a wide range of topics.

The publisher is well known for its popular "Eyewitness" books sold throughout the United States.

The history of the international children's book movement is highlighted by important milestones, some of which we describe in Resource B, Resources for Locating and Learning More About Global Children's Literature, on the companion CD, which lists publishers, organizations, journals, and awards dedicated to international children's literature. You are introduced to Jella Lepman, profiled in this chapter, who established the International Youth Library in Munich, Germany, in 1948, and founded the International Board on Books for Young People (IBBY) in 1953.

In the United States, Mildred L. Batchelder was the driving force in the international book movement. A librarian, she worked at the American Library Association for 30 years and is the namesake for the Batchelder Award (see Resource B on the CD). The American Library Association instituted this award in 1966 to honor the most outstanding translated children's book that was first published in another country.

Perhaps inevitably, more books from the English-speaking countries of the United Kingdom, Australia, Canada, and New Zealand are distributed in the United States than those first written in other languages and requiring translation. In addition, more books are translated from European countries than from other parts of the world. A review of the Mildred L. Batchelder Award recipients since 2000 indicates that three books are from Germany, two from France, two from Japan, two from Israel, and one from Holland.

More recently, since 1971, the Society of Children's Book Writers and Illustrators, a professional organization with over 22,000 members worldwide, has supported the writing and sharing of children's books. Its members include writers, illustrators, editors, librarians, and publishers and booksellers who work in the field of children's literature. In addition to regional chapters within the United States, there are more than 50 chapters throughout the world.

Another important aspect of the international book movement is the international book fairs where publishers share their books. The premier book fair for international children's books is held in Bologna, Italy, in late March or early April. At the Bologna Book Fair, publishers of children's books around the world gather to meet each other, share ideas, and conduct business. These publishers buy and sell rights to books for translation, copublication, and other collaborative arrangements. At the Fair, there are extensive displays and exhibits, awards are given out to books, and speakers share insights. Other book fairs dedicated to children's books occur throughout the world—in Cairo, Egypt; Moldova; Cape Town, South Africa; and for the first time in Dubai in 2010. The Biennale of Illustrations in Bratislava, a prestigious juried exhibition of original international children's book illustrations, takes place biennially in Slovakia. The world's largest book fair, held in Frankfurt, Germany, in October, is also a place where children's publishers exhibit and exchange rights and licenses. In the United States, the annual BookExpo America, held in New York, is a comprehensive publishing event and place for the international buying and selling of children's books.

Global Literature Defined

Careful readers may notice that we have used the term *global* (as opposed to *international*) exclusively. That is intentional, because *global* is arguably more inclusive and probably best fits our definition of global literature. Our view of global literature is that it is *world* literature either set outside the United States or written by persons other than Americans with settings that are unidentified. We only consider books by Americans with clearly identified settings outside the United States as global literature. Thus, literature that is first published in another country (either in English or translated into English) would only be one kind of global literature. As already described, *Jamela's Dress* (Daly, 1999) fits this category.

A second type of global literature is written by immigrants to the United States with settings in their home countries. Peter Sís's (2007) memoir of his experience growing up behind the Iron Curtain in the former Czechoslovakia (*The Wall*) is a good example of this type.

Books written by authors in other countries but originally published in the United States constitute a third variation of global literature. Some of the books by internationally popular Australian author Mem Fox (2000), such as *Harriet, You'll Drive Me Wild*, which was originally published by Harcourt, exemplify this group.

A fourth category consists of books written by American authors with settings in other countries. Jane Kurtz, who grew up in Ethiopia living with her missionary parents, devotes much of her career to promoting literature about that country. Her picture book, *Only a Pigeon* (1997, coauthored with her brother Christopher Kurtz), authentically captures contemporary daily life in Addis Ababa and typifies this kind of global book.

Finally, due to globalization, books in languages other than English and about other countries are more available in the United States (sometimes through independent book sellers or online bookstores) than in the past. We particularly note when these books have English editions or are bilingual texts.

In sum, our definition of *global* literature focuses on books that are *international* either by topic or origin of publication or author. Although we recognize its close connections with multicultural literature, we specifically distinguish global literature from books that portray parallel cultures *within* the United States. Likewise, the goals for global literature, while similar to goals for multicultural literature, extend beyond our national perspective, as addressed next.

Goals for Global Literature

Perhaps Jella Lepman's (2002) goal, for children's books to build bridges of international understanding after World War II, is ultimately most important. If she could sustain that vision arising from the ashes of the Holocaust, one of history's darkest hours, surely it is still worthy and attainable today. Such a bridge from self to others, from the familiar to the foreign, from the near to the far is captured by French literary critic Paul Hazard's (1944) assertion that "children's books keep alive a sense of nationality [and] . . . also . . . a sense of humanity" (p. 146). Thus, literature portrays both what makes every culture unique (or its "nationality") and also what is universal (or our "humanity"). Rudine Sims Bishop's (1994) metaphor of books as "mirrors" and "windows" captures these same concepts and offers two major related goals for the role of global literature.

Figure 1.3	Profile: Jella Lepman

Jella (pronounced *Yella*) Lepman (1891–1970) was the founder of the International Youth Library (IYL) in Germany and a cofounder of the International Board on Books for Young People (IBBY) in Switzerland. Her story began in the aftermath of World War II. The U.S. military came to Lepman to help see to the needs of German children who suffered most from the war. When she returned to Germany for the first time—a Jew, she had fled to England during the war—she wondered what she could do to restore the humanity destroyed by Nazi atrocities. Even though she shuddered at the thought of visiting former Nazi centers, Lepman bravely drove around the ruined streets and buildings in a military jeep with the company of a soldier driver. She visited adults and children affected by the war to see and listen to what was needed most. On her journey, she encountered starving children with no families or homes. They recounted the horror of war without any traces of emotion. Lepman knew that these children needed the power of books to help bring back hope and humanity to their shattered lives.

(Continued)

(Continued)

Jella Lepman envisioned a traveling exhibition of the finest children's books from around the world. Her first challenge was to secure funding for her project. With strong determination, Lepman tirelessly typed letters to European countries requesting children's books for the exhibition. She could hardly contain her happiness when crates of books began to arrive from Switzerland, Italy, Denmark, Belgium, the Netherlands, and other countries. Soon, the books were shelved in a historical building in Munich.

On the opening day, long lines of children streamed through the exhibition building. With beaming faces, children giddily held and leafed through the book collections. In other cities in Germany, the traveling exhibition generated similar enthusiasm. The children couldn't put down the books and begged to bring them home. It became clear to Lepman that the need for a permanent children's book library was urgent. Her idea generated support and donations from abroad, and 1949 marked the establishment of the IYL in Munich. Lepman's vision of establishing a library for the children of war-torn Germany was finally realized. With its international children's literature collection, the library serves to promote cross-cultural understanding.

The IYL project was so impressive that the United Nations invited Jella Lepman to work with children and book experts of many nations to help promote books. She became a world peace ambassador. Children's books allowed her to reach out to many different nations, such as Iran and Turkey. At an international children's book conference in Germany, Lepman and her friends joined together to establish the International Board on Books for Young Children (IBBY) in 1953. Today, Lepman's legacy is still alive. IYL continues to house the international children's book collection and sponsor traveling book exhibitions around the world. Meanwhile, IBBY is dedicated to bringing books to children around the world.

Young readers can learn more about Jella Lepman in *Books for Children of the World: The Story of Jella Lepman*, by Sydelle Pearl (2007). This picture-book biography describes Lepman's efforts to "build a bridge of peace" through children's literature. Lepman wrote about her life in the adult book, *A Bridge of Children's Books* (1964/2002).

—Tati L. Durriyah

One important goal is for literature to offer readers a realistic and authentic mirror of their own lives and experiences. If children recognize themselves reflected accurately and sympathetically in the books they read, they may develop positive self-images and sense of worth. Children need access to books that fulfill these needs, for by self-reflection, they can gain insight and a sense of efficacy. They also can benefit from catharsis by understanding that they are not alone and that others have shared similar experiences. *All* children need a "mirror."

On the other hand, restricting one's gaze to a reflection can be limiting and distorting. Reading *only* about children "like me" teaches readers "to view themselves and their lives as 'normal,' to interpret their own cultural attitudes and values as 'human nature,' and to view other people and other lives as exotic at best, and deviant at worst," cautions Bishop (1994, p. 4). Thus, as a second goal, *all* children need literature that opens "windows" onto lives and experiences that are different from their own. Children's abilities to understand, value, and celebrate diversity evolve from recognizing their places and their particular experiences as part of the universal whole of humanity. Global children's books can support both of these goals.

Conclusion

Stories (both fictional and factual) help humans to organize experiences, to make sense of them, and to learn from them. In fact, narratives are probably the oldest teaching tool in history. We use them to pass on knowledge and wisdom because they capture our imaginations, engage our interest, and enliven our ideas. We innately, it seems, *want* to tell and hear stories, as known by teachers of young children, who exhibit intense desire to share their own life stories! This desire is a powerful motivation for learning.

The strength of stories for learning is not limited to literacy instruction; narratives can enhance learning across the curriculum, as we demonstrate in this book. And, stories are not limited to one genre or even to fiction; biographies, information books, poetry, and folktales contribute their own benefits. Throughout the book, we suggest specific titles to illustrate our points. Remember, for more information about these books (including approximate interest levels), refer to An Annotated List of 341 Children's Books Cited in the Book on the CD that accompanies this text.

As technology advances and opportunities for global communication expand, the value and importance of international children's books will continue to grow. In Part I, we share specific books, curricular connections, and ways to integrate global literature in all areas of the curriculum, beginning with a literary thematic framework.

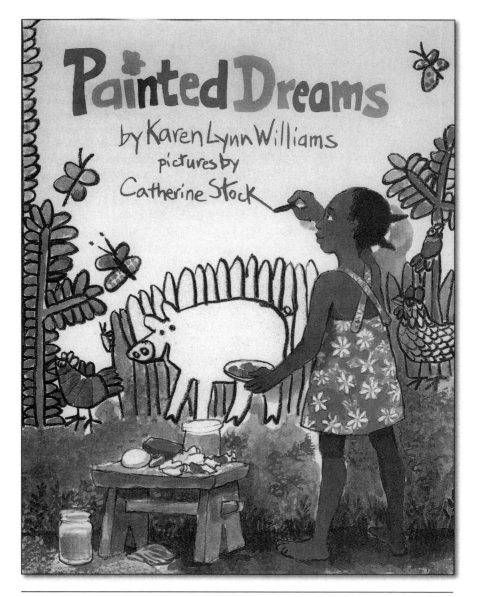

One of the many wonderful children's books described in *Reading Globally, K–8*.

PART I

Infusing Global Literature Throughout the Curriculum

We are the children of Korphe. We live in a village in the mountains of Pakistan. We write in Urdu and English. We add and subtract. We read our books and explore our maps. We are learning in the school that we helped to build. (Mortenson & Roth, 2009)

This passage from *Listen to the Wind: The Story of Dr. Greg & Three Cups of Tea,* by Greg Mortenson and Susan L. Roth, portrays the universal childhood experience of attending school. Yet, the children of Korphe did not have a school until Dr. Greg Mortenson, an American climber, literally "stumbled" into their village after being lost in the mountains and later returned to help the villagers build their own school. Dr. Greg, as he is affectionately called, has now built more than 130 schools in rural regions of Pakistan and Afghanistan. Dr. Mortenson is a strong advocate for educating girls, and 18,000 of the 28,000 students in his schools are girls. He epitomizes the global citizen, an individual who believes that education is a right for all the world's children.

This children's title is based upon Mortenson's (2006) book for adults, *Three Cups of Tea* (coauthored with David Oliver Relin), a highly-rated bestseller on Amazon and one with which many teachers may already be acquainted (see Resource A, Further Recommended Reading for Teachers, on the CD). Imagine the potential for using this book as a stimulus for a schoolwide professional inservice to personalize issues of achieving education against the odds, the need for global perspectives, and the potential for bringing the world to American classrooms through literature. Having set the stage with Mortenson and Relin's book and our opening chapter, you may be ready to embark upon the particulars of how to integrate global literature throughout the curriculum, as we demonstrate in this section. Paul Hazard (1944) offered a useful metaphor for books as messengers from one land to another. Mildred L. Batchelder (1966)—for whom the American Library Association's Batchelder Award for outstanding English-translated children's books is named—likened these books to travelers from one country and language to another. As both messengers and travelers, let's use literature to bring our students to the wider world through reading globally.

2

Literary Theme Studies and an Integrated Curriculum

Young Thembi accompanies her *gogo* (grandmother) to vote in South Africa's first post-apartheid election (in Elinor Batezat Sisulu's, 1996, *The Day Gogo Went to Vote*) and in doing so, witnesses the significance of Gogo's first opportunity to vote in her hundred years of life. This picture book offers rich possibilities for literary discussions in primary grade classrooms and for extending those discussions to relevant, meaningful learning experiences across the curriculum. In this chapter, we first describe a literary framework for teaching with literature and then show how that framework can be incorporated across the curriculum. We next discuss the definition and importance of theme studies and, finally, show how theme studies can integrate curriculum within the literary framework.

A Literary Framework

When teaching with children's literature in elementary and middle school classrooms, always approach books from a literary perspective. Literature can serve many purposes, but its primary value is aesthetic, as a work of art. This requires focusing first on literary qualities and literary responses when we read and discuss litera-ture with our students. A literary framework for teaching and learning helps us to do that. Lehman (2007) fully details this frame-work of literary study, and here we briefly summarize its cycle of three phases.

Phase 1: Reading and Interacting With a Text

The first phase is reading and interacting with books. This might happen through individual reading or the teacher reading a book aloud to a group. In either case, readers or listeners create personal transactions with the text by responding from their background expe-riences and knowledge with thoughts and feelings about what they are reading or hearing. To use the example of *The Day Gogo Went to Vote* (Sisulu, 1996), children listening to this story may have had an experience of accompanying their parents to the polls on an election day. They also may have relationships with grandparents or extended families. These experiences and others may help them to identify with Thembi in this story. They can empathize with the hurt Gogo felt when she was mistreated at the pensions (retirement benefits) office and the sorrow Thembi felt for her gogo's illness. On the other hand, children may be unfamiliar with South Africa and its history of apartheid, vocabulary used in this story, and other cultural aspects. Their lack of knowledge in these areas may raise questions in their minds and can be fruitful topics for a teacher and students to explore together in the next phase.

Phase 2: Sharing Responses With Other Readers

Initial responses lead to the second phase of the cycle: sharing individual responses to literature with other readers. In a read-aloud situation, this phase may even begin while the first phase is still underway; read alouds that invite student discussion during the reading are often called "interactive read alouds." When students read independently, this phase may happen when they engage in group discussions, such as literature circles or while reading and talk-ing with a partner. Either way, this phase builds on Phase 1 by elicit-ing readers' and listeners' past first-hand experiences that help them relate to a character like Thembi or by prompting questions about new material.

For example, in one second-grade classroom, when the children first heard this story, they had difficulty placing the time period, as it was before they were born. Students also asked about the story setting—South Africa—and whether it was real. However, they related Gogo to their own elderly grandparents and great-grandparents and their health concerns. They connected the application of ink on Gogo's finger when she voted to stamps they had received on their hands at amusement parks. Some children worried that someone would try to hurt Gogo voting, and they expressed interest in the car that conveyed her to the polls, a Mercedes Benz. In hearing each other's responses, thoughts, and questions such as these, children's personal insights are enriched and shaped by multiple perspectives. Thus, the community of readers constructs mutual meanings, which become the basis for the third phase of the cycle.

Phase 3: Making Connections That Promote Literary Growth

Making connections that promote literary growth, the last phase, usually requires more direct involvement from teachers with a strong literary perspective and foundation. Again, this phase can begin while either of the first two phases are ongoing or sometimes through follow-up learning experiences. To continue with the *Gogo* example, when children share their past experiences, a teacher can attach these to larger themes, such as the importance in our lives of loving intergenerational and extended family relationships, our need to feel important and special, or the joy of celebrating a special occasion. A teacher can help students explore the characteristics displayed by Thembi or her gogo, such as having determination, courage, curiosity, and pride. The story's township setting, largely portrayed through Sharon Wilson's pastel illustrations, can be examined, and questions for future exploration can be generated. Unfamiliar terms offer rich opportunities for building children's language repertoires.

Finally, to help students connect this story more closely with American experiences *and* to develop intertextuality (or connections among texts, which can enhance comprehension), a teacher may pair the book with *Papa's Mark*, by Gwendolyn Battle-Lavert (2003), a picture book that depicts an African-American man's first experience with voting in the post-Civil War South. For example, in the second-grade class described above, children had heard *Papa's Mark* before being introduced to Gogo, and they immediately made connections between the two. They remembered the word *gogo* from having heard Niki Daly's (1999, 2002, 2004, 2006) Jamela books, and they connected Gogo's traumatic treatment at the government pensions office to the beating of the young girl in *White Socks Only* (Coleman, 1996).

Figure 2.1	Classroom Vignette: Paired Reading Promotes Global Connections (Grades K-5)

Ms. Givens briefly introduced two books, *Once Upon a Time,* by Niki Daly (2003), and *Thank You, Mr. Falker,* by Patricia Polacco (1998), to a group of four third-graders. She handed out a simple graphic organizer with two columns, each with a book title and the subtitles: Beginning, Middle, and End. Ms. Givens asked the group to write down what happens in each story as they read to compare to them. A few days later, Sharon came excitedly to the group discussion and started to share her response before Ms. Givens could even finish asking a question.

Sharon: . . . I have a connection because I was very, very bad at reading, but once I did reading club it helped me just a little and then now I'm very . . . (laughing)

Ms. G: This year you've become very good. Don't you think?

Sharon: (nodding) Mm-hum. I wanna read, I wanna read better . . .

Paired reading not only helps students like Sharon make personal connections with stories, but it also can help children expand their thinking and talk about different perspectives on themes, characters, and structures (Lehman & Crook, 1998). For example, in the following discussion, students noticed that protagonists' problems and bully figures are similar in both books. The students diagnosed Trisha's problem as being more serious than Sarie's because Trisha is much older. They also put themselves in Trisha's shoes and felt for her.

Dani: . . . I would say her [Trisha] in [*Thank You Mr. Falker*], that Trisha had a way bigger problem . . .

Sharon: Yeah.

Dani: . . . than Sarie.

Ms. G: Why?

Dani: Because what you said about starting fifth grade, like it should already be, like you should be good at it. I think that since she is still like really bad at it that . . .

Matt: I'll be embarrassed . . .

Dani: Yeah, I'll be very embarrassed.

Matt: . . . if I couldn't read in fifth grade.

In particular, even though the setting in *Once Upon a Time* was unfamiliar to them, they had no problem making connections between their lives and Sarie's life in South Africa. This unfamiliar international book was understood easily when it was paired with *Thank You, Mr. Falker,* the students' home-country book (Freeman, Lehman, & Scharer, 2007).

Afterwards, Sharon exclaimed what a great discussion it had been! In fact, during the entire discussion, Sharon was engaged and demonstrated clear comprehension of both books. She liked being able to talk based on her own experiences. She hid her pride behind a shy smile as she said this, and I knew that paired reading had proven to be an effective tool that could be used with virtually any student.

Teacher: Dona Givens, Grade 3, Dublin, Ohio

Writer: Jongsun Wee, Columbus, Ohio

Such interconnections can initiate a new literary cycle: Phase 1, reading and interacting with books; Phase 2, sharing individual responses to literature with other readers; and Phase 3, making connections that promote literary growth. Interconnecting cycles begin to weave a broader "tapestry" (Oxley, 1995) of literature as a whole. Such intertextuality also provides useful launching points to other areas of the curriculum, as we demonstrate next.

Incorporating the Framework Across the Curriculum

Literary study, such as just described, can extend across the curriculum and, thus, greatly expand the amount of time in busy school schedules for such learning. That is, while we are teaching skills or information, we can do so in a *literary* manner (Lehman, 2007); we can fulfill curricular benchmarks while engaging in literary study. (In the following discussion, we highlight literary concepts.) To continue with *Gogo* (Sisulu, 1996), a teacher can ask children, while reading or listening, to use the context of the story to predict the meanings of unfamiliar terms and thereby draw attention to the story's *language*. Then, the words' definitions can be checked in the book's glossary and lead to further inquiry on the Internet or in other books. For example, the website http://isizulu.net provides a definition for *gogo*, and readers of the Jamela books (cited in Chapter 1) will discover that she also lives with her gogo.

Furthermore, *Gogo* (Sisulu, 1996) introduces readers to Nelson Mandela respectfully, as *tata*, or father. Because Mandela was indeed a father of the new South Africa, a class can discuss the term's *symbolism* in a manner that even young children can grasp. Interested readers will find more information about Mandela in a biography, such as the picture book by Floyd Cooper (1996), *Mandela: From the Life of the South African Statesman*, or Chris van Wyk's (2009) picture-book version of *Nelson Mandela: Long Walk to Freedom*. American students can compare his *character*, in addition to his historical importance, to that of an African American leader in the Civil Rights Movement, such as Martin Luther King, Jr., about whom there are many fine biographies for young readers. Comparisons of the struggles to overcome segregation in the United States and apartheid in South Africa can help students to understand the larger significance of the two leaders' work. These important issues relate to literary *themes* of striving to overcome adversity and realizing one's dreams.

Examining a globe or world map can help children gain a better grasp of *setting*—and may result in outright amazement that two such distant settings could produce many similar circumstances.

Thus, while learning new information about South Africa and applying skills, such as using reference tools or maps, students also can learn about language, symbolism, character, themes, and setting. Furthermore, as one can see, from this expanding web of investigation, larger studies around several potential topics or theme studies can emerge.

Theme Studies

A theme study usually begins with a topic, such as apartheid in South Africa or American civil rights, and develops that topic into a theme about the topic. The distinction is that while a topic is limited to a few words, a theme explores deeper, underlying meanings about that topic and is a more literary concept (Lehman, 2007). For example, a broad theme about the topics cited above might be equal rights for all people are a universal human desire and right. More specifically, the struggles to end apartheid in South Africa and ensure civil rights in the United States share important similarities, as well as some differences. Good literature, through the power of narrative, can make such hefty themes appropriate for primary-grade students and engage them in substantive investigations. (Picture books may also be a good tool for introducing literary concepts to older readers in preparation for reading more advanced texts. For professional resources on this topic, see Benedict, 1992, and Tiedt, 2000.) Another theme that might resonate with young children who hear or read about Thembi's life is that, in spite of the obvious differences in location, Thembi experiences the same feelings that our students may have had (about accompanying an adult on an important task, sharing a special love with grandparents, or celebrating a major event with one's family and neighbors). Identification with Thembi also develops readers' empathy for her.

Any of these themes (and additional possibilities) can form the basis for a thematic unit, composed of related learning opportunities that explore selected aspects of the core theme. If we go with the theme identified above—the struggles to end apartheid in South Africa and ensure civil rights in the United States share important similarities—we could begin with the meanings of *apartheid* and *segregation* and what they involved. We could delve into how they originated in South Africa and the United States, respectively, and compare historical timelines of these practices and their dismantling, anchored by the lives of famous leaders or heroes in each situation. We could investigate a link that both Mandela and King shared with Mohandas Ghandi, who first (as a young lawyer) led the struggle for Indian rights in South Africa (parallel to the struggle for Black rights there) and later embodied nonviolent resistance to British rule in his native India. His model of civil disobedience inspired the movement led by King in the United States. We could read Leonard Everett Fisher's (1995) picture-book biography, *Gandhi*, to learn more about this great leader, which might launch us into a study of India and its movement to attain independence.

If we want to pursue the other theme mentioned above—the universality of Thembi's feelings for her grandmother—we could link with another story from South Africa, *Not so Fast, Songololo*, by Niki Daly (1985). Here, a young boy accompanies his gogo on a shopping trip to the city. In return for his help, Gogo buys him a beautiful new pair of red *tackies* (sneakers). Songololo feels important and proud to help his grandmother (feelings similar to Thembi's) and surprised and happy with his new shoes. We could connect these stories thematically to those of other children sharing loving relationships with grandparents around the world, such as *Babu's Song*, by Stephanie Stuve-Bodeen (2003), set in Tanzania; *Saturday Sancocho*, by Leyla Torres (1995), set in Colombia; or *Grandfather Counts*, by Andrea Cheng (2000), and several of Patricia Polacco's stories based upon her own family, all set in the United States. Again, each of these stories could naturally lead to further explorations across the curriculum, as we discuss next.

Figure 2.2 Profile: Niki Daly

Niki Daly—of Irish, English, and Afrikaner descent—is probably the most widely known author-illustrator outside of his native South Africa. In 1985, he gained international acclaim with the publication of *Not So Fast, Songololo*, considered to be the first picture book published in then apartheid South Africa to depict an urban black child protagonist (and later developed into a video by Weston Woods Studios). Since then, his series of books about the indomitable Jamela (*Jamela's Dress*, 1999; *What's Cooking, Jamela?* 2002; *Where's Jamela?* 2004; and *Happy Birthday, Jamela*, 2006) have earned him a loyal following of young readers around the world. *A Song for Jamela* (2009) is the latest title in the series.

(Continued)

(Continued)

However, Daly has been writing and illustrating his own and other authors' books since 1978, with *The Little Girl Who Lived Down the Road,* published while he was living in London, where he had gone to pursue a career as a singer and songwriter. There, he met and married his wife, Jude Daly, an accomplished children's book illustrator in her own right, had a son (the Dalys now have two grown sons), and the family decided in 1979 to return to South Africa at the height of apartheid to be part of the change that finally came to that country a decade later.

Daly's early interest in cartoons and caricatures is evident in his style of illustrating, and he characterizes himself as a "drawer" rather than a "painter." His confidence as a writer developed later and has blossomed with a novel for primary- to intermediate-grade readers, *Bettina Valentino and the Picasso Club* (2009), illustrated with his own drawings. Across his work, certain themes emerge, such as childhood imagination, creativity, and play (sometimes even leading to trouble!); engaging in common childhood experiences, such as an outing with a *gogo* (grandmother); and dealing with worries and even dangers (having an alcoholic father or being menaced by a stranger), but always with hope.

Daly has used his own prominence as an artist to promote the work of other authors, illustrators, and indigenous children's book publishing. He convinced David Philip Publishers to launch the Songololo Books imprint, which he helped to edit, and has advised many budding writers and artists regarding their own careers. He particularly hopes to see more black writers for children in South Africa, whose voices he believes are still underrepresented. Daly also believes that children's books have spanned and will continue to bridge racial divides in South Africa and promote healing—not by offering heavy-handed messages, but by simply portraying positive, realistic images of all types of people. This is the goal for his own work and his hope for the future of children's literature in South Africa.

Niki Daly lives in the same suburb of Cape Town where he was born, in a historic cottage that became the setting for the home into which Jamela, her mother, and grandmother move in *Where's Jamela?* (2004). This neighborhood has changed dramatically from being all white during his childhood to a vibrant, multicultural, bustling, if perhaps slightly unkempt community in which people of many nationalities live, work, and commute every day—a perfect image of the new South Africa.

—*Barbara A. Lehman*

Integrating the Curriculum

Lauritzen and Jaeger (1997) make a compelling case for the possibilities of narrative to integrate learning across the curriculum. They state that "story is the most meaningful context for making sense" (p. xiv), or constructing meaning. In addition, we believe that such integration can produce better transfer of learning to novel situations and can encourage flexible thinking. Thematic units, implemented within a literary framework, can accomplish this integration. As noted by Pappas, Kiefer, and Levstik (2006), thematic units "link together

content from many areas of the curriculum and depict the connections that exist across disciplines" (p. 68). (For a relevant example of
how a thematic unit becomes a "literary tapestry" that weaves
throughout the curriculum, see Peggy Oxley's, 1995, account of her
second graders' engagement with the theme, "Strangers in a Strange
New Land: A Study of Migrations.")

We have already shown how children's literature can lead to further explorations through more reading. Now, we return to those
ideas and add others to demonstrate explicit curricular integration
(with subject areas highlighted). Attention to language is the heart of
language arts, and discussion of unfamiliar terms in *Gogo* (Sisulu,
1996) or any of these books promotes language arts learning. *Saturday
Sancocho* (Torres, 1995) not only contains new terms, but the separate
Spanish edition invites language comparisons between the two texts.
Grandfather Counts (Cheng, 2000) extends language learning to
Chinese. Further, we also can ponder how the use of such languages
enhances the themes of these stories; specifically, in *Grandfather
Counts,* counting in Chinese and English becomes the means for a
grandfather and granddaughter who speak different languages to
begin a relationship. Finally, when we link to biographies of famous
people, we can study features of different literary genres, that is, realistic fiction and biography—a language arts standard, as we discuss
in Chapter 3.

In the area of *geography,* we use maps to locate the settings of these
books, both fiction and nonfiction. We apply *mathematics* if we calculate the distances of those places from us. We use *history* to study
apartheid, civil rights, or independence movements (like India's) and
math, again, to construct timelines of this history. If we want to read
more about segregation in the United States, we can read historical
picture books, such as *White Socks Only* (Coleman, 1996) and *Sister
Anne's Hands* (Lorbiecki, 1998), biographies, such as Nikki Giovanni's
(2005) *Rosa* and Robert Coles' (1995) *The Story of Ruby Bridges* or Ruby
Bridges' (1999) personal account, *Through My Eyes*. A discussion of
voting ties with *civics* or *government* lessons, enhanced by nonfiction
titles such as Eileen Christelow's (2003) *Vote!* and *America Votes: How
Our President Is Elected,* by Linda Granfield (2005). All of these experiences further the goals of *multicultural education* as we learn about
different cultures around the world and within the United States.

Technology can enhance our studies in any of these areas, as we
search the Web for resources from books to videos to lesson ideas and
for information on countries, languages, or famous people. On the
Internet, we can find exciting photographs, films, or other visuals and

hear music or speeches from the places we study. We can extend children's responses to books we have read or have them present new knowledge gained by incorporating writing, drama, and art activities; software technology can facilitate these processes. Discussion of relationships with grandparents around the world could lead to interviewing older people and gathering oral histories. Video recorders can capture these interviews, and students can word process their reports or present them through multimedia formats. These reports could be posted on a class webpage. Students could have e-pals with a class from another country we are studying and share with them their thoughts and ask questions about books they are reading in common. (To learn about e-pals, check www.epals.com, a website for school use that claims to have participants from 200 countries and territories.)

Some readers (especially teachers in upper elementary or middle school grades) may think that curricular integration works only in the primary grades. After all, they may teach only one subject in a departmentalized situation. We recognize that integration may take more effort in such contexts than in a self-contained classroom, but we believe that it is possible. More importantly, we agree with Siu-Runyan and Faircloth (1995) that older students *need* integrative learning to meet their unique early adolescent developmental needs. Teachers can plan as teams across subject areas, creating complementary lessons that relate the thematic study to their content and that demonstrate connections between disciplines, which these students may otherwise fail to grasp. To facilitate this, schools can be creative with their scheduling—combining language arts and social studies teaching into larger blocks of time, for example. (To find out from other middle school teachers how block scheduling works for them, visit the website www.middleweb.com/INCASEblkschd.html.)

Some readers also may be thinking that the book examples used in this chapter are aimed toward primary grades. This is deliberate, as our experience and research (Scharer, Freeman, Lehman, & Allen, 1993) has indicated that teachers of younger children may appreciate assistance when it comes to literary study, while feeling more confident addressing literacy skills or specific content knowledge. Therefore, we wanted to demonstrate clearly that a literary focus is *not* incompatible with literacy or content orientations and to support primary teachers in making this connection.

However, the same principles—using a literary framework and incorporating it with theme studies to integrate the curriculum—apply to upper elementary and middle school grades. For example, a middle school class discussion of a Batchelder Award winner such as

Samir and Yonatan, by Daniella Carmi (2000), could evolve into a larger study about cross-cultural friendships. This novel could be related to Jane Kurtz's (1998) *The Storyteller's Beads* about two Ethiopian girls from different religions (Jewish and Christian) who put aside their mutual distrust and fears to help each other survive and escape from oppression in their homeland. We could connect those books to an American context by adding Mary Ann McGuigan's (1997) *Where You Belong,* set in 1963, about an interracial friendship between two girls in a Bronx neighborhood of New York City. Cross-cultural friendships is an important topic in global literature that can become a deeper theme of young people overcoming traditional views of "us and them" and offering hope for reconciliation. This theme can be extended through informational texts, such as *No More Strangers Now: Young Voices From a New South Africa* (McKee, 1998) or Deborah Ellis's (2004) *Three Wishes: Palestinian and Israeli Children Speak* and Lauri Dolphin's (1993) *Neve Shalom/Wahat Al-Salam: Oasis of Peace.* The theme would also naturally involve cross-curricular inquiries in history and geography, have relevance for current events, and no doubt extend into additional subject areas, as well.

Conclusion

Thus, we believe that teachers at all grade levels can help students learn both skills and subject material through a literary framework. Such teaching does require teachers to first approach a book for its literary qualities and not immediately leap into the *lessons* we may want students to learn. Curricular benchmarks *will* be achieved while we are thinking *literarily. The Day Gogo Went to Vote* (Sisulu, 1996) is important for more than what we can learn about the transformation of South Africa or the importance of voting. It is fundamentally an engaging story about an old woman and her young grandchild sharing a momentous experience together. Chapters 3 through 6 provide more details and ideas for cross-curricular global literary encounters.

3

Integrated
Language Arts

Ali loves writing the letters of his language: "I love to make the ink flow—from my pen stopping and starting, gliding and sweeping, leaping, dancing to the silent music in my head" (Rumford, 2008). *Silent Music: A Story of Baghdad* (2008) is a first-person account of Ali's desires to create calligraphy much like his "secret hero," Yakut, who lived in Baghdad over 800 years before. Yakut fled to a high tower during the attack by Mongols in 1258, and there he "shut out the horror and wrote glistening letters of rhythm and grace." Similarly, Ali found comfort in writing as the bombs and missiles fell in his beloved city in 2003. "I wrote all night and the many nights of bombing that followed. I filled my room with pages of calligraphy. I filled my mind with peace."

Global children's literature offers rich opportunities for children to grow as passionate readers and writers, like Ali. Books like this provide windows into the lives of others and should be central to language arts instruction. This chapter focuses on the ways global literature supports instruction in the integrated language arts, defined by the International Reading Association (IRA) and the National Council of Teachers of English (NCTE) in the *Standards for the English Language Arts* as "a curricular organization in which students study and use the language components of speaking, listening, reading, and writing as a mutually reinforcing process that evolves through a unified core of concepts and activities" (1996, p. 49).

IRA/NCTE Standards for the English Language Arts

The IRA/NCTE (1996) *Standards for the English Language Arts* were developed during a four-year, federally funded project involving educators from across the United States. The standards are based upon research and theory of how students learn, particularly how students learn language (see http://www.ncte.org/standards). The 12 listed standards are described as interrelated with opportunities for the "innovation and creativity essential to teaching and learning" rather than endorsement of a particular curriculum or program of instruction (IRA/NCTE, 1996, p. 3). This chapter is organized around four standards particularly salient to the role of global children's literature in integrated language arts instruction:

1. Standard 1 focuses on reading a wide variety of texts about the United States and the world;

2. Standard 2 emphasizes learning about a variety of genres written in many different time periods;

3. Standard 5 centers on developing writing skills to use within a range of purposes and contexts; and

4. Standard 9 requires students to develop a deep understanding of diverse cultures, language, dialects, ethnicities, and geographic regions.

Just as the 12 standards are interrelated, the books and suggestions offered in this chapter will overlap with other books and activities and clearly align with multiple standards. We hope that the following books and ideas will support the exciting, creative teaching practices the standards assume.

Standard 1

Students read a wide range of print and nonprint texts to build an understanding of texts, of themselves, and of the cultures of the United States and the world; to acquire new information; to respond to the needs and demands of society and the workplace; and for personal fulfillment. Among these texts are fiction and nonfiction, classic and contemporary works. (IRA/NCTE, 1996, p. 3)

Reading aloud books of many genres with students every day is an excellent instructional tool to meet this standard. A more recent term, "interactive" read aloud (Fountas & Pinnell, 1996), is used to describe the read-aloud experience that involves students in conversation before, during, and after the story. A teacher carefully selects just the right text with the students in mind to support their discussion and foster learning. To start an interactive read aloud, the teacher and students may discuss the book's cover, or connections with the book's author or illustrator, or think about questions they have about the book's content. As the teacher reads and shares the illustrations, children know that their comments are valued; they are expected to share their questions, comments, or wonderings about the text and illustrations as the book is read. The teacher may plan several times for students to talk with their neighbor to share their thoughts about the story or reply to an open-ended question the teacher has posed. Or, the teacher may mark several places in the book to invite a group discussion about the plot, characters, content, themes, or illustrations. After the reading, students may respond through discussion, shared writing, or individual writing to help them think more deeply about what they have just heard.

The youngest readers enjoy books that invite them to participate. *Ten Little Fingers and Ten Little Toes,* by popular Australian author Mem Fox (2008), celebrates the commonalities of babies no matter where they are born. Babies born on the ice or far away in a tent "as everyone knows, had ten little fingers and ten little toes." Fox's rhythmic text invites young readers to join the refrain that is printed in the book large enough to be seen by a small group in a shared reading context. For a larger group, the teacher could write the refrain on sentence strips or chart paper and point to each word as the children read along. Your class can listen to Mem Fox read the book at http://www.memfox.com/mem-sings-a-book.html.

Figure 3.1   Profile: Mem Fox

Mem Fox is Australia's most highly regarded author of picture books. Her first book, *Possum Magic* (1983), is the best-selling children's book of all time in Australia. Her best selling book in the United States is *Time for Bed* (1993), a bedtime lullaby for very young children. Two of her most popular books in the United States are *Wilfrid Gordon McDonald Partridge* (1984) and *Koala Lou* (1988). *Wilfrid* is a touching story about a small boy who helps his elderly friend find her lost memory. *Koala Lou* is about a young koala who yearns to hear her busy mother tell her, "I DO love you." Many of Fox's picture books are short pattern books, such as *Where is the Green Sheep?* (2004), and are excellent choices for shared reading experiences and for class books based on the patterns of the stories.

Fox maintains an extensive website where students can discover that she loves world peace and a clean kitchen sink and loathes identical letters from a class and brown clothes. Students can also listen to Fox read aloud some of her picture books. Although she has been a highly successful writer for many years, readers may be surprised to learn that Mem Fox considers writing picture books to be a great challenge because the text must be precise and succinct.

In addition to writing picture books, Mem Fox also writes nonfiction books for adults. She is passionate about literacy and reading aloud. In *Reading Magic* (2001), the author extols the power of reading aloud to young children. In her book she describes how reading aloud promotes literacy: "The fire of literacy is created by the emotional sparks between a child, a book, and the person reading" (p. 10). On her website (http://www.memfox.com/welcome.html), the author offers 10 read-aloud commandments, for example: "1. Spend at least ten wildly happy minutes *every single day* reading aloud."

Mem Fox was born in Melbourne, Australia, in 1946. She spent her childhood in Zimbabwe, where her parents were missionaries. Fox was a teacher educator for 24 years and is now retired from Flinders University, South Australia. She spends her time as an international literacy consultant and is very active in the promotion of peace around the world. Her picture book, *Whoever You Are* (1998), brings children the message that no matter how different we may look from one another, we all laugh and cry; joy and love are the same the world over. Fox lives in Adelaide, Australia with her husband, Malcolm. Daughter, Chloë, is a politician in South Australia.

Fox has written more than 30 picture books; a recent title is a fairy tale, *The Goblin and the Empty Chair* (2009). According to a video interview, Fox believes that "It's very, very important that children have fairy stories that are confusing, frightening, and end up happily" (Apnicommunity.com, 2006).

—Lisa D. Patrick

Also suitable for shared reading with a small group, Ole Könnecke's (2006) *Anthony and the Girls* has been translated into English by Nancy Seitz from the original German version. With brief text at the bottom of each page, the slightly oversized book offers an engaging story of Anthony's amusing attempts to join the girls who are playing in the sandbox. The story ends with a twist, and this unresolved ending is perfect for talking and writing about what might happen next.

Figure 3.2 Teaching Idea: Writing a Sequel (Grades K–3)

Ole Könnecke's *Anthony and the Girls* (2006) ends as Luke arrives with hopes of joining Anthony and the girls in the sandbox. Thus, readers are left wondering what will happen next—a great opportunity for writing a sequel! Before writing about what might happen next, you'll want to discuss with the class the key elements of the story that inform the sequel. For example, the girls ignored Anthony as he tried to get them to notice him. Will they also ignore Luke? Anthony tried valiantly to gain access to the sandbox and was only successful because of the girls' sympathy after his injury. Will Anthony share his hard-earned space in the sandbox or expect Luke to work hard to join the three friends? As the class decides on answers to these questions, make notes about their ideas that will support their writing either as an interactive writing (with the teacher sharing the pen with the children), a shared writing (as the teacher writes what the class composes), or as individual stories, written by each student, shared, and finally compiled into a class book.

Selecting books with similarities to read aloud also can support the interactive nature of reading aloud as children begin to make connections across texts. For example, a teacher could begin by reading aloud *Hannah Duck* by Anji Yamamura (2008). Hannah Duck lives peacefully with her friends Gigi the parakeet and KameKame the turtle except for Sundays, the day she wanted so much to walk through the park but was too frightened to enter. *Chibi: A True Story from Japan* (Brenner & Takaya, 1996) is also about a duck in Japan and based on a true story of a mother duck and her 10 babies who lived in an office park in downtown Tokyo. The littlest duckling was named Chibi (tiny) by a local news photographer. Discussion of these two books could lead, of course, to the reading of Robert McCloskey's (1941) classic *Make Way for Ducklings* as well.

| Figure 3.3 | Teaching Idea: Comparing Books Across Countries (Grades 1–5) |

The following books are excellent opportunities to look for similarities and differences across books and countries: *Hannah Duck* by Anji Yamamura (2008), *Chibi: A True Story From Japan* (Brenner, 1996), and Robert McCloskey's (1941) classic, *Make Way for Ducklings*. Any one of the books could be read aloud to students first and discussed in terms of literary elements such as plot, setting, or illustrations. When the second book is read and discussed in a similar way, the class could begin to think about connections across the texts in terms of both similarities and differences. Students could make their own charts to document their thinking and use their charts to contribute to a class chart. After reading the third book, each student could select a favorite and write a rationale for selecting that one special book. Results could then be made into a graph and displayed along with students' writing and accompanying illustrations.

A wide array of books celebrating the alphabets of countries around the world also make good read-aloud choices. *A is for the Americas*, by Cynthia Chin-Lee and Terri de la Peña (1999), moves across South America, Central America, and North America with each letter touching on different celebrations, food, sports, homes, and locations. In contrast, Barbara W. Klunder (2009) chose to focus on one island close to Toronto, Canada, in *The Animals' Day: An Island Alphabet*. What if, the author proposes, the animals on Toronto Island threw a party once a year? Each two-page spread offers brief text in alphabetical order with a pinch of alliteration and a small watercolor illustration framed in white. The horses find hats to come in handy; jays make jarring jazzy notes; and the rascally rats and raccoons need to be restrained! The small size of the book will make reading to a large group challenging, but it is a lovely excuse to move in close to appreciate the illustrations! Readers interested in Klunder's art can visit her Web-based gallery at http://www.barbaraklunder.com/. Much information about African life is found in *An African ABC* by Jacqui Taylor (2001). The top of the left page of each spread features a letter of the alphabet embellished with related animals, plants, and objects, which are featured in the largely alliterative text below. The right side has a full-page illustration including everything mentioned in the text framed in white with the letter in each of the four corners.

Interactive reading aloud is not just for primary students but should be part of the upper grade curriculum, as well. Two chapter books about the struggles of growing up in Cuba and the Dominican Republic are a likely pair to read aloud in succession. The main character in *The Color of My Words*, by Lynn Joseph (2000), is a 12-year-old girl who lives in a poor village near the sea in the Dominican Republic. Ana Rosa is a poet and a writer who uses her words to come to grips with the challenges of life in her village. The text alternates between poetry and first-person narrative as readers learn more about the difficulties faced by Ana Rosa, her family, and community. Eduardo F. Calcines' (2009) *Leaving Glorytown: One Boy's Struggle Under Castro* is also written in first person as an autobiography of Calcines' childhood in Castro's Cuba. Calcines' experiences are both well-written and shocking and provide important insights into this important time period in Cuba. Visit http://glorytown.net/ to learn more about the author and his work.

Teachers who sometimes worry about the amount of time it takes to read a chapter book to students should consider the benefits of providing a fluent, expressive model and access to books that students may find difficult to read or understand independently. An interactive read aloud is the perfect opportunity to monitor comprehension based on students' responses and to provide support when understanding weakens. Another benefit is the potential for reading chapter books to encourage greater independent reading. For example, students who listen to the reading of one Suzanne Fisher Staples novel set in India, Pakistan, or Afghanistan may head to the library for more. Another possibility is that students will become interested in life in Pakistan after listening to *The House of Djinn* (Staples, 2008) and select books like Amjed Qamar's (2008) *Beneath My Mother's Feet* and Padma Venkatraman's (2008) *Climbing the Stairs*, each about the experiences of young girls in social contexts quite difficult for females. Thus, the time spent reading aloud is also an investment in other aspects of a reader's life.

| Figure 3.4 | Teaching Idea: Global Author Studies (All Grades) |

This chapter introduces many award-winning authors and illustrators such as Suzanne Fisher Staples, Emily Arnold McCully, Mem Fox, Ed Young, Diane Stanley, Anno, and Minfong Ho. Reading their books is a natural way to begin an author or illustrator study, either as a class or in small groups. Students could research the backgrounds of the authors or illustrators for insights into their craft and use the Internet to find websites created by the authors or illustrators and also reviews of their work. Collecting as many books as possible for the study will enable students to experience the range of topics and techniques in the set and deepen their understanding of the authors or illustrators by reading and thinking across many different books. Keep a class list or chart of characteristics of each author or illustrator, adding to the chart as new books are read.

Reading aloud picture books in the upper grades provides for shorter stories typically enhanced with illustrations not found in chapter books. Books that cross countries offer insights into the immigrant experience for older students. *Manjiro: A Boy Who Risked His Life for Two Countries* is a true story by Emily Arnold McCully (2008) about a 14-year-old Japanese boy who was saved from a fishing boat wreck by the captain of an American whaling ship and his experiences in California during the 19th-century Gold Rush and eventual return to his homeland. Set in a similar time period, *Oranges on Golden Mountain*, by Elizabeth Partridge (2001), begins in China as Jo Lee's mother makes the painful decision for him to sail to the United States to fish with his Fourth Uncle, so there will be enough food for his little sister.

Reading or listening to books such as the ones above provide "windows" (Bishop, 1994) for students to learn about the world in important ways that contribute to this standard. They will learn more about themselves and others, how to respond to the needs and demands of the global society, and find personal fulfillment.

Standard 2

Students read a wide range of literature from many periods and in many genres to build an understanding of the many dimensions (e.g., philosophical, ethical, aesthetic) of the human experience. (IRA/NCTE, 1996, p. 3)

Many works of fiction in picture-book and chapter-book formats are included in every chapter of this book. For teachers seeking informational books, Chapters 4 and 5 offer a wealth of recommendations. Given that attention to fiction and nonfiction, we will focus on several other genres to discuss this standard. First, we explore poetry in a variety of formats with the full range of types of poems available for readers of all ages. Then, we discuss biographies and autobiographies, which not only provide insights about people around the world but also people from long ago.

Global Poetry

Poetry books with diverse formats and designs are available for today's readers and listeners. Some are collections like *No Hickory No Dickory No Dock: Caribbean Nursery Rhymes*, written and remembered by Guyana natives (now living in Britain) John Agard and Grace Nichols (1995), with vibrantly colored scratchboard illustrations by Cynthia Jabar. Listeners will enjoy the variations of rhymes familiar in the United States like "Humpty" as well as the circular, concrete poems of the "Skipping Rope Spell" and counting rhymes like "What Turkey Doing." Jane Yolen's (1992) collection of *Street Rhymes Around the World* shares playful games from 17 different countries, demonstrating the universality of play across cultures. In the introduction, Yolen explains that rhymes in languages not written in Roman alphabet letters are provided in their original language as well as in "a phonetic translation or *transliteration* of the words so you can 'hear' how these rhymes sound." Jan Greenberg's (2008) *Side by Side: New Poems Inspired by Art From Around the World* is also a collection of both poetry and art organized around four themes—stories, voices, expressions, and impressions—and features two-page spreads of art and poetry written in both the original language and translated into English. This format invites discussion of the meaning of each poem relative to the art selected by Greenberg.

Minfong Ho's (1996) *Maples in the Mist: Children's Poems From the Tang Dynasty* is a step back in time to the Golden Age of China, 618 to 907 AD. Ho explains in the translator's notes that these were some of the poems she learned as a child that "stirred in me a curiosity about and a pride in Chinese culture." She translated the poems, printed in both English and Chinese, in hopes that future generations of children will also come to love them "in one long unbroken chain." A more contemporary collection in the format of a counting book is found in *One Leaf Rides the Wind*, by Celeste Davidson Mannis (2002). The setting of the book is a Japanese garden where a young girl is enjoying its beautiful features—two carved temple dogs, five roofs of the pagoda, and eight pond pillows. A haiku is offered for each number along with a full-page oil painting by Kathleen Hartung and special notes below explaining a bit more about each part of the garden.

These collections offer important opportunities for word play as children ask for them to be read over and over, savoring the sounds and making their favorites part of their memory to recite and share with others. Favorites can be written on sentence strips or chart paper for shared reading and entered into each child's personal poetry notebook along with illustrations revealing the child's understanding of the poem and its cultural context. Young poets will enjoy *Troy Thompson's Excellent Peotry Book,* originally published in Australia by Gary Crew and Craig Smith (2003), as an example of how they can collect their poetry assignments, favorite poems, and responses from their teacher into a single personal book. Between the brown paper bag endpapers, this book offers a wide range of poems of many genres in a scrapbook-like format. Some of the poems and responses by his teacher are quite humorous, like his collection of limericks; others are more serious like "The Ballad of Sergeant Thompson" that tells the story of the night Troy's father was killed by "street scum."

Other books focus on a single poem. *Bean Soup (Sopa de frijoles),* by Jorge Argueta (2009), who spent most of his life in El Salvador, is an illustrated cooking poem written in both Spanish and English. Each page offers a step or two in the process of making bean soup with illustrations by Columbian artist Rafail Yockteng showing a boy's efforts to prepare the delicious dinner for his family. This book makes a wonderful companion for Lulu Delacre's (2000) *Salsa Stories,* as the main character collects stories by family members from Guatamala, Cuba, Puerto Rico, Argentina, Mexico and Peru, which are each linked to family recipes in the last half of the book. These books offer important opportunities to relate two different genres and formats with a single theme.

Figure 3.5   Teaching Idea: Poetry Slam (All Grades)

The poetry books and collections in this chapter can be the beginning of a classroom collection read across the year. When students are familiar with many poetry books in their classroom, they find it enjoyable to read favorites again and again. Every few weeks, your class can prepare for a "Poetry Slam"—a time when students share favorite poems they have prepared for the audience. Getting ready for this time means that students will pore over poetry books to pick just the right poem and read it over and over to perfect the intonation, phrasing, and expression that will support the meaning of the poem. Collect the poems into a class book that can be read and enjoyed over and over. Great fun and fluency practice too!

Elephants Never Forget! is written by Anushka Ravishankar (2008), also known as "India's Dr. Seuss." The story rhyme is full of excitement as a young elephant is separated from the herd during a storm and finds a new family in a herd of water buffalo. Many pages offer sound words like *Squish, Splosh, Ccrrrack, ROAR,* and *BELLLOOOW* making this book a wonderful introduction to onomatopoeia. Mark Reibstein (2008) combines prose and original haiku to tell the story of *Wabi Sabi,* a cat in Japan looking for the meaning of her name. Each page also offers decorative Japanese haikus by Basho and Shiki from the 17th and 18th centuries, which are translated into English at the end of the book. Visit http://bookscreening.com/2009/07/16/wabi-sabi-by-mark-reibstein-illustrated-by-ed-young/ to see a YouTube interview with the author explaining where he got the idea for the book and with Ed Young in his studio and the author with his cat that inspired the book.

Two other examples of global poetry in fascinating formats are biographies of famous poets. *The Poet Slave of Cuba,* by Margarita Engle (2006), is a biography of Juan Francisco Manzano told in chapter book format. Each brief chapter is a poem from the perspective of either Manzano or an important person in his life. The life and poetry of Japanese poet, Basho, are offered for listeners of all ages in Dawnine Spivak's (1997) *Grass Sandals: The Travels of Basho.* Like *Wabi Sabi,* the story line is punctuated with examples of Basho's poetry as well as Japanese characters of a salient word for that phase of his travels.

Biographies: People Near and Far, Now and Long Ago

Picture-book biographies written by Diane Stanley and Peter Vennema of famous international people of the past like Leonardo DaVinci, Michelangelo, Peter the Great, Joan of Arc, Shaka King of the Zulus, and, most recently, Mozart, are widely available in the United States. Some are both written and illustrated by Stanley; others are cowritten with Peter Vennama, like the 1994 picture book, *Cleopatra.* If multiple copies for each title are available, students can select a favorite and work in small groups to learn about both the person and the genre. Sharing with the entire class is an opportunity for comparison across books and may inspire readers to check out additional titles and conduct further research about an individual from the past.

Another way to organize a study of biographies would be through a theme—like famous writers. The study might begin with Raquel Benatar's 2003 bilingual story of the life of the famous contemporary Chilean writer, Isabel Allende, in the book, *Isabel Allende: Memories for a Story (Isabel Allende: Recuerdos para un cuento).* The text on the left offers Spanish at the top and English at the bottom, with insights into Allende's mystical childhood experiences in her grandmother's house "full of books, spirits, and eccentric relatives," which influenced her writing talents and topics as an adult. The study might then step back in time with picture books about famous authors such as Shakespeare and Dickens. Diane Stanley and Peter Vennema (1993) teamed to write *Charles Dickens: The Man Who Had Great Expectations*. Like Allende, Dicken's talents as a writer were heavily influenced by his childhood experiences in 19th-century England working in a boot polish factory, pasting on labels, and living by himself in a cheap boarding house.

Walter Dean Myers's (1999) *At Her Majesty's Request: An African Princess in Victorian England* links Europe with West Africa. The biography begins in what is present-day Nigeria as a village is attacked, and a young girl is captured by the followers of King Gezo and presented to Queen Victoria as a gift from the "King of the blacks to the Queen of the whites" (p. 14). Myers based the book on a set of about 50 letters that he purchased in a London rare books store, photos acquired through the Royal Archives, and excerpts from Queen Victoria's diary. Older readers can appreciate the research required to piece together such a story and may be inspired to do their own research to write a biography of someone else. To learn more about Myers's work visit http://www.walterdeanmyers.net/.

We close this discussion of biographies with an autobiography by Uri Shulevitz (2008), *How I Learned Geography*, based on a time, early in his life, when his family had fled from Poland to Turkestan (now, Kazakhstan) to escape the dangers of World War II. When his father brings home a map, Uri finds himself transported to places all over the world. Through his imagination, he visited sandy beaches, snowy mountains, and fruit groves full of papayas and mangos.

It is exciting to see the wide range of global literature available in so many genres and topics that can be shared with students to meet the expectations of Standard 2. Books such as these truly offer opportunities to learn about many dimensions of the human experience.

Standard 5

> Students employ a wide range of strategies as they write and use different writing process elements appropriately to communicate with different audiences for a variety of purposes. (IRA/NCTE, 1996, p. 3)

This standard, while not specifically linked to our definition of global literature, is crucial to the definition of language arts in terms of students as writers. Global literature offers important learning opportunities for supporting students as they increase their abilities as writers. One way is for quality books to become "mentor texts" for children as writers. Scharer (2007) writes, "skillful immersion in enjoyable texts, followed by thinking about the writing, enables children to use these texts as 'mentors' that will help them in their own writing" (p. 124). Some young writers enjoy writing new variations of familiar stories or poems. *The Empanadas That Abuela Made* (*Las empanadas que hacía la Abuela*), by Diane Gonzales Bertrand (2003), is a variation of the familiar rhyme "The House That Jack Built." The cumulative text in both English and Spanish builds to tell the story of a happy Abuela who feeds the family by rolling the dough to make pumpkin-filled empanadas. Students could also create variations as a group as the teacher writes their text on chart paper during shared writing, which then becomes a favorite text for reading aloud.

First-person narratives are often the genre children find most comfortable as they tell stories about their own lives and experiences. Young writers may find the format of *I Live in Tokyo* (Takabayashi, 2001) to be an interesting way to write about experiences across a year. The first few pages of this book by Mari Takabayashi introduce the main character, a little girl, telling about her life in Japan month by month. Then, each two-page spread is dedicated to one month. Brief paragraphs at the bottom of most pages explain the month's activities, and illustrations are labeled to support understanding. Revisiting this book as part of a writing minilesson to look closely at the author's techniques could inspire children to write their own book, using the months of the year as a framework.

Other books support children as they learn about letter or journal writing about traveling to other places. *Around the World: Who's Been Here*, by Lindsay Barrett George (1999), begins with a letter to a class from their teacher who will be traveling on a ship for nine months as part of a Circumnavigation-of-the-Globe Grant. The teacher's letters to the class from various places around the world each end with the question, Who's been here? which is answered on the following page. James Rumford (2001) places text inside a road that moves across each two-page spread to tell the story in journal format of *Traveling Man: The Journey of Ibn Battuta, 1325–1354* from Morocco. The roads intersect at times with boxes of longer narrative to tell the story of Battuta's adventures across Africa and Asia. Both books offer children opportunities to improve their own writing if guided by the teacher to think in terms of the decisions the writers made. They also are good examples for students to learn about the travelogue genre.

What's Going On?, originally published in Barcelona and written by Elena O'Callaghan (2008), is an excellent example of how to build up suspense to a surprise ending. Through the voice of a young boy, readers get glimpses of each member of the family "before" and "now." Although this book is clearly intended for the younger child, picture books like this can also inform more mature writers, when examined in terms of the writer's craft, to study a succinct example of writing with spare text, allowing for and expecting inferences on the part of the reader. Similarly, writers studying how to develop a character in their stories would benefit from the writing of Mathilde Stein (2007) in *The Child Cruncher*, originally published in the Netherlands. The three characters—a little girl, her father, and the child cruncher (a big, ugly villain)—are not what you would expect. Quite bored, a little girl is thrilled when captured by the villain, and her father tells her to have fun! Illustrations by Mies van Hout make significant contributions to character development, as well, by picturing the villain ironically resting with a small stuffed rabbit and the preoccupied father busy working at his computer.

Students and teachers can study the author's craft, the characteristics of various genres, the techniques authors use, and the masterful language they hear and read to accomplish Standard 5 through global literature. This will support them as writers who know how to communicate in a range of different ways, depending on the purpose and audience for their writing.

Standard 9

Students develop an understanding of and respect for diversity in language use, patterns, and dialects across cultures, ethnic groups, geographic regions, and social roles. (IRA/NCTE, 1996, p. 3)

All the literature and teaching ideas in this book contribute to this standard. As children see their teacher intentionally select books from around the world, identify books that are translations, and introduce authors and illustrators worldwide and where they live, students will begin to develop both an understanding of and respect for diversity from a global perspective. We now focus on one more genre, folklore, and explore its contribution to this standard.

Variations of folktales are one of the most common ways that global literature is found in today's schools. Teachers often collect versions of the "Cinderella," "Red Riding Hood," or trickster tales. Children's literature texts, like *Charlotte Huck's Children's Literature,* by Barbara Kiefer (2010), offer lists of books to enhance any teacher's collection. An author study, such as the works of Demi, is rich in folklore through books like *The Magic Pillow* (2008) and *The Greatest Treasure* (1998) and support conversations across books as children learn more about Chinese culture with each book shared. Studying the work of Demi is also an opportunity to closely examine the illustrations from her trademark use of gold, to more subtle uses of Chinese motifs and themes across books.

Figure 3.6	Classroom Vignette: A Book Comparison Using International Folktales (Grades K–2)

When doing a book comparison including international literature, I have found it's a good idea to begin with the most familiar story. For this comparison, I first read Trina Schart Hyman's (1983) Caldecott Honor book *Little Red Riding Hood*. This selection contains features that American children would traditionally recognize, including the characters, the setting, and the plot.

As I read *Little Red Riding Hood,* I stopped to ask several prediction questions. Natural points are when Little Red Riding Hood is setting out from home, after she has met the wolf, and after the grandmother and/or girl are swallowed by the wolf. I could tell from the discussion that these questions enhanced the students' understanding of the story.

Next, I introduced students to the international selection, *Pretty Salma: A Little Red Riding Hood Story From Africa*, by Niki Daly (2006). I read the book title, discussed the cover illustration, and asked a prediction question about where students think the story takes place. We also located Ghana, West Africa, on our classroom map and globe. This helped students begin to visualize the world in which they live. I read the story, stopping again throughout the book to ask questions supporting discussion.

After the two books were read, we were ready to engage in a book comparison. I did this using a pocket chart in the shape of a Venn diagram, although a three-column chart is another excellent way to complete the same task. Title the Venn diagram or three columns with Little Red Riding Hood, Both, and Pretty Salma. When doing this learning activity with kindergarten students, I wrote ideas from the story on word cards (e.g., *girl, wolf, dog, grandmother, huntsman,* and *grandfather*). As this was the first time I had done a book comparison, I first explained the sorting task to the students. Then, I read one of the ideas and asked students where they thought that word should be placed on the chart and why. After placing the word cards that were prewritten, I asked students to name other similarities and differences that we then added to the chart.

The book comparison activity crossed several days, catering to young children's short attention span and providing times to revisit the stories looking for more ideas. Engaging students in higher level, critical thinking tasks such as a book comparison helps them notice more detail in a story than if they had heard only one version. When using global literature, students' lives are expanded from what is most familiar outward to the world beyond.

Teacher: Barbara Irwin, Kindergarten, Shauck, Ohio

Maranke Rinck's (2008) version of "The Blind Men and the Elephant," *I Feel a Foot!* was first published in the Netherlands. The story is set in the dark of night as five animals, sleeping in a hammock together, hear a rustling noise and try to find out what's making the noise from their own perspectives. The friends are certain that they have a whopper of a Tur-Bat-Octo-Bird-Goat until elephant laughs and reveals himself. The elephant joins the friends in the hammock but suddenly hears something, leaving the end of the tale up for discussion and debate.

In Nancy Raines Day's (1995) *The Lion's Whiskers: An Ethiopian Folktale,* Fanaye tries to earn the love of her stepson, but the loss of his mother is so painful that he rejects her every attempt. This book pairs nicely with *Pulling the Lion's Tail*, by Jane Kurtz (1995), about a young Ethiopian girl who tries to win the affection of her new stepmother and learns a similar lesson. Classroom suggestions for this and other books by Kurtz, who grew up in Ethiopia, are found at http://www.janekurtz.com/books/pulling.html.

Legends are tales relative to a specific time in history or location that are believable but not necessarily true (Kiefer, 2010). Margaret Musgrove (2001) went to Ghana on a Fulbright Grant to research *The Spider Weaver: A Legend of Kente Cloth*. Two men find an extraordinary web of beautiful colors and try to take it home to study, but the fragile web is destroyed as they try. Visit http://www.pocanticohills .org/kente/kente.htm to see a second-grade class responding to this book by making their own kente cloth designs.

Alice Provensen (2001) retold and illustrated two Chinese legends in *The Master Swordsman & The Magic Doorway: Two Legends From Ancient China*. Both are stories of trickery, learning, and overcoming adversity. In the first, a young boy, Little Chu, travels long distances to find Master Li in hopes he will learn swordsmanship. The title of *The Magic Doorway* foreshadows the ending of the story as the emperor plans to execute the painter when he has completed his mural so that no one can have a painting as wonderful as his own. However, when he finally completes the mural, the painter uses the blue door he has incorporated into the painting to escape because "I have some more paintings to make, and I cannot make them without a head."

It is fitting to end with this standard, as all of the books in this text contribute to Standard 9 so that "students develop an understanding and respect for diversity" (IRA/NCTE, 1996, p. 3). Students' worlds are often small, rarely extending beyond their home, school, and community. Global children's literature brings the world to them and is central to the development of an international perspective on diversity.

Conclusion

The books in this chapter all contribute to one or more standards for teaching and learning in the English language arts. They are rich in opportunities for oral language development, learning new vocabulary as well as an appreciation of the writer's craft. Teachers do not need to find a separate time for global literature; rather, the time for global literature is during every subject, every day. In Chapter 4, we demonstrate how appropriate global literature is for teaching social studies.

4

Social Studies

We all know that there are lots and lots of people in the world—and many more millions each year . . . . Each and every one of us different from all the others. Each one a unique individual in his or her own right. (Spier, 1980)

Three decades ago, Caldecott Medalist Peter Spier (1980) wrote and illustrated *People*, an amazing compendium praising diversity while also affirming the universals that bind the world's people together. This one informational picture book presents a global perspective and supports all ten of the thematic strands in the national social studies standards. Students of all ages enjoy this book with its humorous, detailed illustrations that provide a motivating way to introduce any of the curricular strands.

Social studies is a vast, integrated subject in the curriculum which draws on the disciplines of anthropology, archaeology, economics, geography, history, law, philosophy, psychology, religion, and sociology. According to the National Council of the Social Studies (n.d.), "the primary purpose of social studies is to help young people develop the ability to make informed and reasoned decisions for the public good as citizens of a culturally diverse, democratic society in an interdependent world" (Introduction, para. 3). In 1994, NCSS approved the Curriculum Standards for the Social Studies, which are organized around 10 thematic strands: culture; time, continuity, and change; people, places, and environments; individual development and identity; individuals, groups, and institutions; power, authority, and governance; production, distribution, and consumption; science, technology, and society; global connections; and civic ideals and practices. The social studies standards indicate that "students should be helped to construct a *global perspective* that includes knowledge, skills, and commitments needed to live wisely in a world that possesses limited resources and that is characterized by cultural diversity" (NCSS, n.d., para. 31). Global literature naturally supports this goal of the social studies curriculum.

This chapter demonstrates how global literature can be incorporated in social studies instruction. We share two topics, one for primary and one for upper elementary and middle school, that support multiple standards. Then we explore two of the curriculum strands, one for primary and one for upper elementary and middle school students. Next, we describe ways that the genre of biography and memoir and their relationship to culture can be integrated into the curriculum. Finally, we discuss books that specifically promote international peace and justice (a fundamental goal of international literature).

Topic 1: "Wake Up World"

(Primary Grades)

This topic derives its title from the book, *Wake up, World! A Day in the Life of Children Around the World* (Hollyer, 1999) and focuses on similarities among children regardless of where they live as well as the unique features of their culture. In the book, young readers meet eight children from around the globe. Color photographs show these young people as they engage in activities that most children share, like waking up, starting their day, and going to school. The text and photos establish each specific cultural context, so readers can learn about the differences that also exist. For example, in the section on "Helping Others," we learn that Anusibuno in Ghana sweeps and fetches firewood, while Sasha in Russia collects water from the well by pulling "heavy canisters on a sled." This book is published in association with Oxfam, and all royalties support Oxfam International, a group of 13 organizations working to eliminate poverty and injustice. Students could learn more about this international charity and its efforts at www.oxfam.org.

Two other books also focus on universal experiences of childhood. In *Children Around the World* (Montanari, 1998), first published in Italy, 12 fictional children from diverse countries are introduced through text and colorful multimedia artwork. Each double-page spread features one of the children with first-person text describing the child's life. Students could select one of the children and create a Venn diagram comparing their life with that of the child in another part of the world. As noted in Chapter 2, teachers can arrange for individual student or class pen pal exchange through www.epals.com.

A second book, *The Milestones Project: Celebrating Children Around the World* (Steckel & Steckel, 2004), features quotes and photographs from children around the world as they discuss milestones such as birthdays, pets, and school. In this title, international children's authors and illustrators have also contributed messages. The unique characteristics of the format can be discussed as a mentor text, and children can write their own thoughts about one of the milestones to create a class book. Teachers can consult the website www.milestones project.com for additional information and resources. According to the website, the project's "immediate goal is to reduce prejudice, intolerance and hatred" (Milestones Project, 2010, para. 1), and it received the 2003 Global Peace and Tolerance Award by the Friends of the United Nations.

With these three books as an introduction, primary students might next read titles that focus on a child's life in a specific culture and provide more in-depth understanding of the cultural context. In *Torina's World: A Child's Life in Madagascar*, author-photographer Joni Kabana (2008) provides a pictorial journey with Torina, who narrates each photograph and poses a question to the reader. For example, a photograph shows adolescent boys pulling people in a cart. The text reads, "We get rides in the pousse-pousse. What do you ride in?" Children can use the pictures to determine the meaning of *pousse-pousse* and to learn more about life in Madagascar. Children also learn, for example, that "Madagascar is the world's fourth largest island." After locating Madagascar on a world map, children can discover the three larger islands in the world, where they are found, and how they might compare with Madagascar.

British photographer Prodeepta Das transports children to Janla, India to meet six-year-old Geeta and her family in *Geeta's Day: From Dawn to Dusk in an Indian Village* (1999). Students can create a timeline of what Geeta does during the day and compare it to their own daily schedule. If there are children in the school who are Indian American, a parent or grandparent could be invited to class to share childhood recollections of growing up in India. Specific vocabulary, introduced in this book, could lead to an in-depth discussion of these words or concepts. For example on one page, three games that Indian children play are illustrated: ha do do, chaka chaka bhaunri, and puchi, which is Geeta's favorite. Children could locate more specific instructions from other resources, such as the Internet, and then play these games.

| **Figure 4.1** Teaching Idea: Puppetry in Response to "Wake Up World" (Grades 1–3) |

After children have learned about the daily lives of peers around the world, they can select a child from another country and create a puppet representing the child. Classroom teachers can partner with art teachers on this project to assist students in crafting their puppet. In small groups, students can present a puppet show to describe and reenact the lives of children around the globe. Students may invite another classroom and/or their parents to view the puppet show.

Through "Wake Up World," the social studies curriculum strands of culture, people, places, and environments; individual development and identity; and global connections are all being supported. In the next section, a topic for upper elementary and middle school students will be described.

Topic 2: World War II and the Holocaust

(Upper Elementary/Middle School)

World War II and the Holocaust are topics taught in the upper elementary grades and middle school. A myriad of books representing all genres are available for young people, but we feature books that were either first published in another country or present a little-known perspective on the topic.

Four-time Batchelder recipient and Hans Christian Andersen award winning author Uri Orlev from Israel has written historical novels based on his own and others' experiences in Poland during World War II. Two of these books, *The Island on Bird Street* (1984) and *The Man from the Other Side* (1991), are set in the Warsaw Ghetto where Orlev lived for part of the war. In a third title, *Run, Boy, Run* (2003), a young boy escapes from the Warsaw ghetto. A film version of *The Island on Bird Street*, produced in 1997 by First Look Pictures, is available on DVD. The main character in each book is a boy based on an actual person and true experiences. If the class was divided into three groups with each group reading one of the books, students could then compare and contrast their main characters, the plots of their stories, and the themes, engaging in literary study as described in Chapter 2. Students can also read the chapter "In the Warsaw Ghetto" in Michael Leapman's *Witnesses to War: Eight True-life Stories of Nazi Persecution* (1998), a book from Great Britain, and conduct their own historical research to find out more about the Warsaw ghetto and its uprising. Students could research other historical ghettos to determine why these were created and how ghetto life impacted inhabitants.

Figure 4.2	Profile: Uri Orlev

Books by Israeli author Uri Orlev have received the Mildred L. Batchelder Award more times than any other author's. In 1985, *The Island on Bird Street* (1984) was named the winner, followed by *The Man from the Other Side* (1991) in 1992, *The Lady with the Hat* (1995) in 1996, and *Run, Boy, Run* (2003) in 2004. These four books share themes that relate to the Holocaust. All Orlev's books are written in Hebrew and have been translated into English by Hillel Halkin.

Born in 1931 in Warsaw, Poland, Orlev was the son of a Jewish doctor; his given name was Jerzy Henryk Orlowski. During World War II, his mother, a chemist, was killed by the Nazis, and his father was a Russian prisoner. Orlev and his brother lived with their aunt in the Warsaw Ghetto, were hidden by Polish families, and then spent two years at the Bergen-Belsen concentration camp until it was liberated by the Americans. He and his brother were reunited with their father in Israel in 1954. While at Bergen-Belsen, he wrote 15 poems in Polish in a notebook that survived the war. In 2005, Orlev translated these into Hebrew and they were published under the title *Poems from Bergen-Belsen, 1944.*

Orlev has been writing children's books since 1976 and has penned more than 30 books, although only a handful of them have been translated into English. They have, however, been translated into more than 35 languages. Many of his books are based on true experiences that occurred during the Holocaust. In his acceptance speech for the Hans Christian Andersen Award, which he received in 1966, he said, "The Holocaust was simply part of my childhood, and just as the childhoods of writers, painters, musicians, and movie makers are frequently a source of inspiration for them, so has mine been for me. What has motivated me all my life is the need to tell stories, which lead to more stories and to connections between people of different ages and cultures" (Glistrup, 2002, p. 94). One way that Orlev coped during his childhood experiences was to imagine he was the "hero of a thriller who had to survive until the happy ending on the book's last page, no matter who else was killed in it, because he was the main character" (Orlev, 1997, p. 31).

In addition to writing books for children, Orlev has translated Polish books into Hebrew and has written scripts for radio, television, and movies. His books have received numerous national and international awards, including Germany's Best Audio Book for Youth in 2006 and the 2003 Premio Cento Award, Italy's prize for outstanding children's book, both for *Run, Boy, Run* (2003). A movie based on *The Island on Bird Street* debuted in 1997.

Orlev lives in Jerusalem, is married, and has four children and several grandchildren. In an article based on a personal interview, Freeman (1999) concludes, "My visit to Uri Orlev's home was an inspiring time for me . . . . My inspiration results from the realization that, not only is his ability to bring compelling, universally appealing stories to children admired internationally, Uri Orlev is a man of warmth, courage, humility, and hope" (p. 47).

—*Evelyn B. Freeman*

The country of Denmark stood strong against the Nazis and had an active resistance movement. In the Batchelder Award-winning book, *The Boys from St. Petri* (Reuter, 1994), a group of high school boys engage in their own acts of resistance against the Nazis who have occupied their country. This exciting novel, based on actual events, demonstrates how ordinary young people can show courage and patriotism in the face of persecution. Danish-born Sandi Toksvig (2007), now living in Britain, has written *Hitler's Canary*, which approaches the resistance through the eyes of 10-year-old Bram and his theatre family. The entire family participates in facilitating the Danish resistance. These novels can be paired with books about the Danish resistance written by U.S. authors: Lois Lowry's (1989) Newbery Medal book, *Number the Stars*; Ellen Levine's (2000) informational book, *Darkness Over Denmark: The Danish Resistance and the Rescue of the Jews*; and the picture book, *The Yellow Star: The Legend of King Christian X of Denmark* (Deedy, 2000). Students can visit the website of the Danish Resistance Museum in Copenhagen http://www.nationalmuseet.dk/sw23424.asp to find out more information about what might have motivated an entire country to resist Nazi occupation, face dire personal consequences, and rescue the country's Jewish population.

In 1938, the Refugee Children's Movement in England organized the first *Kindertransporte* of Jewish children from European countries to Great Britain. Canadian author Irene Watts (1998, 2000) has penned two historical novels, *Good-bye Marianne: A Story of Growing Up in Nazi Germany* and its sequel, *Remember Me*, based on her own experiences as an eight-year-old child who left Berlin in 1938 on the Kindertransporte. A PG-rated Academy Award-winning documentary, *In the Arms of Strangers: Stories of the Kindertransport*, is available on DVD and includes a study guide for grades 7–12. Students can compare *Kindertransport* accounts to the experiences of American orphaned and homeless children who were sent from New York City to Midwestern families between 1854 and 1929. Andrea Warren's (1996) *Orphan Train Rider: One Boy's True Story* would be a good companion book to foster such discussion.

Inge Barth-Grözinger (2006), a teacher in Germany, has penned the novel *Something Remains*, based on actual incidents in the small town of Ellwangen, Germany, during the early years of Hitler's rise to power. Twelve-year-old Erich Levi is a bright, popular, happy boy from a prosperous, highly respected Jewish family. When Hitler comes to power, Erich's life begins to change, as he and his family encounter anti-Jewish policies, discrimination, and abuses until they are forced to leave the town that they love and emigrate to the United States. This book presents a balanced perspective as it includes strong characters of all ages who continue to stand by the Levis, even as they face negative repercussions. The book describes how a community can alter its fundamental values, the way it treats its citizens, and how traditions and history can radically be transformed—all fodder for engaging discussions with middle school students.

Several recent informational picture books present perspectives on the Holocaust that are little known. In *The Grand Mosque of Paris: A Story of How Muslims Rescued Jews During the Holocaust* (Ruelle & DeSaix, 2009), readers learn how the Muslim community in Paris helped to rescue Jews during the Nazi occupation by hiding them in the Grand Mosque of Paris. The afterword documents the authors' research to write the book and concludes, "It seems that many of the details of this story are destined to remain forever uncertain, with few facts proven to a historian's satisfaction" (p. 35). This book provides evidence of the close historic relationship between Muslims and Jews that is important to remember in light of the current struggles in the Middle East. It also prompts discussion of historical research and may inspire students to undertake their own historical investigations.

Another nonfiction account of a little known incident is *The Secret of Priest's Grotto: A Holocaust Survival Story* (Taylor & Nicola, 2007). In 1993, Christos Nicola, an experienced caver, found artifacts in the Priest's Grotto cave in the western Ukraine. His curiosity led him to discover the story of three families who escaped Nazi persecution and survived the war by living in the underground cave for 344 days. Color photographs document the survivors' stories and the cave's conditions. This book is a testimonial to perseverance, loyalty, and hope. It also describes how Nicola followed clues to solve the mystery of the cave's inhabitants, thus providing a model for the inquiry process.

All the books discussed in this section highlight efforts to resist Nazi persecution by Jews, Muslims, and Christians. They promote a hopeful viewpoint on how people demonstrate courage and bravery to cooperate in challenging times. A topical study of the Holocaust and World War II supports the curriculum strands of "Time, Continuity, and Change," "Power, Authority and Governance," and "Global Connections." In the next section, we explore how one of the social studies curriculum strands can be taught in the upper-elementary grades and middle school.

Curriculum Strand: Individual Development and Identity

(Upper Elementary/Middle School)

This social studies curriculum strand explains, "personal identity is shaped by one's culture, by groups, and by institutional influences" (NCSS, n.d., Thematic Strands, para. 10). In novels with global settings, child protagonists often confront moral dilemmas and search to find their own identity. Children in the United States, who struggle with similar emotions and situations, can identify with these main characters. Yet, they can also learn how the specifics of one's culture and environment can shape the nature of these dilemmas and impact how the child protagonist may respond.

Figure 4.3	Classroom Vignette: The Storycard Project: Exploring Culture in Conflict and Transition (Grades 3–8)

As an educator seeking to bring global and cross-cultural literature into the classroom, my eighth-grade language arts classes presented me with a real challenge. We were nestled in a rural suburb merely an hour from New York City, yet our community reflected little cultural diversity. Only a handful of students had traveled overseas; "foreign" books were not part of our literary landscape. Threads of Italian-, Irish-, German-, Russian-, and Polish-American cultures were visible; however, people of color were a scant minority, leaving the cultural fabric a mottled beige. Some students identified with a particular thread while others saw remote connections; many felt no cultural identity. How could I help my students relate to the dynamics of culture, an abstract and sometimes alienating concept? The answer came in a picture book with an international setting by Japanese-American writer/illustrator Allen Say (1999).

Tea with Milk helped our class explore culture, not as a fixed *product,* but as an active *process* often in conflict and transition. Say relates how his mother, Masako, felt isolated and rejected in the United States when her parents emigrated back "home" to Japan. Masako saw herself as an outsider, struggling to reconcile the aspects of American culture she enjoyed with the traditional ways of her Japanese heritage. The book's title symbolizes the tension, giving a concrete metaphor to illustrate her preference for blending a traditional Japanese practice (drinking tea) with the tastes she came to appreciate in California (adding milk).

As a class, we read the text aloud then discussed the theme of culture in conflict and transition. The crisp writing, rapid pace of the story, and clear plot in this picture book enabled my classes to address an abstract concept with ease. We then applied the ideas raised through literature to begin the story card project where students would write about how they saw culture in conflict and transition throughout their community. Each student would contribute an approximately 200-word story to be shared among all five of my language arts sections. I allotted one class period to read the book and discuss the project. For homework, students interviewed friends and family members and wrote a brief proposal. Over the next three periods, we used computers to write, edit, format, and print each story on half of a standard 8½" × 11" sheet of white card stock. The text was formatted so that, when folded, each story would be printed on the inside of a table tent. Many students illustrated the front of the card; all were encouraged to write a metaphorical title similar to *Tea with Milk* that would capture the cultural tension and intrigue readers.

Storycard examples included The Florijersian, surprising contrasts of living between Florida and NJ; Shalom, Bonjour, two languages, one conversation; and The Fil-Am, a brother's journey to America becomes part of this student's pride and history. Students remarked how much they learned about their community and classmates. Overall, use of a global picture book combined with the story card project sparked the kind of broad and inclusive discussion of culture I had hoped.

Teacher: James Stiles, Grade 8, Glassboro, New Jersey

In *Naming Maya* (Krishnaswami, 2004) 12-year-old Maya visits her mother's native India to sell her grandfather's house after his death. Set in Chennai, India, where the Tamil language is spoken, and written in the first-person, the story reveals Maya's struggles and frustrations. For example, she indicates, "A mother and daughter should be a team. It isn't that way with us. We don't understand each other" (p. 8). In addition to discussing universal emotions of preadolescents, students can learn about Chennai, India, the Tamil language (a glossary of Tamil words is included), and Hindu traditions.

Another 12-year-old in a different part of the world also struggles with self-identity as well as questions of loyalty and moral dilemmas. In *Sacred Leaf* (Ellis, 2007), Diego has escaped enslavement by illegal cocaine merchants and found refuge with the Ricardo family, who has grown and sold the coca plants for hundreds of years. As the author's note explains, "coca is a sacred plant to the indigenous people of Bolivia—one of the poorest countries in the Western hemisphere" (p. 202). Yet, the American war on drugs has pressured the Bolivian government to halt the growing of the crop, which also is the main ingredient of cocaine. Students recognize Diego's moral dilemmas and a different perspective on how the U.S. war on drugs may have unanticipated negative consequences in another culture.

The question of loyalty can be further explored in *Burn My Heart* (Naidoo, 2007), set in Kenya in the 1950s. The friendship between Matthew Grayson, an 11-year-old white boy whose prosperous parents own land on which 13-year-old Mugo and his family work, is tested when rebellion against British colonial rule breaks out in Kenya. The Mau Mau movement considered the land controlled by whites unlawfully taken from the blacks. Naidoo presents the perspectives of both boys, enabling readers to understand the complexities of deciding what is right and to explore multiple moral dilemmas experienced by both of them. Students can discuss the question, Whose land is it? and compare through research the situation in Kenya to that of Native Americans in the United States.

Figure 4.4 Teaching Idea: Comparing Two Books From Kenya (Grades 4–6+)

The novels *Burn My Heart* (Naidoo, 2007) and *The Mzungu Boy* by Meja Mwangi (2005) are both set in British-ruled Kenya in the 1950s, when the Mau Mau Rebellion is leading the fight for independence. Both titles also involve an interracial relationship between two boys and offer fruitful comparisons. After reading the two books, the teacher and class together could construct a T-chart for making comparisons in setting, characters, point of view, theme, plot, and authors. Such a chart would reveal similarities and differences that could serve as the basis for discussion. Alternatively, the chart could be developed in small discussion groups that could report to the class, leading to further comparison between the groups' charts.

The themes of loyalty and friendship are also developed in the Batchelder Award-winning fantasy, *The Thief Lord* (Funke, 2002). In this novel, orphaned brothers Prospero and Bo escape from their cruel aunt and uncle and find refuge in a Venice theater with a group of homeless children whose 13-year-old leader, Scipio, is known as the Thief Lord. A fast-paced adventure story, the book prompts many questions for students to discuss. Why might children decide to live on their own rather than in an unhappy home setting? What did you learn about loyalty and friendship? Why did Scipio hide his true identity? Students will also want to investigate more about the integral Venice setting.

Figure 4.5 Profile: Cornelia Funke

Cornelia Funke (pronounced Foon-ka) has sold more than ten million children's books worldwide, and is the author of more than 40 titles, 14 of which have been translated into English. While she doesn't mind when people call her "funky," some book critics have called Funke "The German J. K. Rowling," not only for her popularity, but also for her contribution to the genre of fantasy for young readers. Among Funke's renowned translated works are middle grade fantasy novels *The Thief Lord* (2002); *Dragon Rider* (2004); and the Inkheart trilogy, *Inkheart* (2003), *Inkspell* (2005), and *Inkdeath* (2008). Popular worldwide, *Inkheart* was released as a motion picture in January 2009. In 2006, *The Thief Lord* also was adapted into a film version.

Funke concedes that she did not write her first book until nearly the age of 35. Born in 1958, and raised in the small town of Dorsten, Germany, she says that it took her a long time to determine what she wanted to do in life. According to her website (www.corneliafunke.de), Funke initially studied education because she wanted to work with children. Later, she began a social work career and maintains the greatest respect for the profession. Feeling compelled to employ her artistic talents, however, Funke took up book illustration and subsequently became a designer and illustrator of books for children. Although she enjoyed her new work, she yearned to illustrate stories that included magical worlds, dragons, and sea serpents. So she decided to write her own stories, all of which have been appealing to publishers.

It is perhaps thanks to an 11-year-old bilingual (German-English) fan of Funke's novel *Herr der Diebe (The Thief Lord),* first published in Germany in 2000, that Funke's work was introduced to British editor Barry Cunningham, currently of Scholastic Books. The young girl wrote to Cunningham, who also discovered J. K. Rowling, to inquire why *Herr der Diebe* was not available in English when, in her opinion, it was better than Harry Potter. Cunningham took the letter seriously and in 2002 published the English translation, *The Thief Lord,* which immediately made the *New York Times* bestseller list for more than 25 weeks. The translation also won a Mildred L. Batchelder Award, the Book Sense Book of the Year Award, and many other honors. Set in Venice, Italy, Funke says this book, which tells the story of a gang of homeless children, was inspired by her experience as a social worker.

The English translations of *Dragon Rider* and the *Inkheart* books soon followed, each novel residing on bestseller lists for weeks. For younger readers, Funke also developed the Ghosthunters series (2006–2007), which features slime-filled adventures that are both scary and silly, and a picture book, *The Princess Knight* (2001). While Funke always creates her stories in German, today she works and lives in Los Angeles, California, with her son, daughter, and dog. Luckily for her fans, she plans never to stop writing!

—*Denise Davila*

These four books, all with protagonists between 11 and 13 years old are set in diverse parts of the world. Yet, each main character struggles to find personal identity and confronts various dilemmas. Readers come to realize that "what is right" may have many shades of meaning and that situations can be viewed and interpreted from multiple perspectives, depending on the context. In the next section, we turn our attention to the primary grades and the curricular strand of "Individuals, Groups, and Institutions."

Curriculum Strand: Individuals, Groups, and Institutions

(Primary Grades)

This strand is described in the standards as "Institutions such as schools, churches, families, government agencies, and the courts all play an integral role in our lives" (NCSS, n.d., Thematic Strands, para. 18). The institution of school is appropriate to select as a basis for exploring this strand in the primary grades. American children generally take free, public education for granted, as it is considered a fundamental right in the United States. Yet *school* is a concept with many layers of meanings as it is understood around the world. Teachers can introduce the topic by sharing the UNICEF book first published in the United Kingdom, *A School Like Mine* (Smith & Shalev, 2007). Colorful photographs show children and their schools on all continents, and U.S. children will become aware that school often means something different for children in other parts of the world. For instance, Safaa lives in Abu Sir, Egypt, a community about 20 miles from Cairo. Only girls attend her school which meets from Saturday to Wednesday. Reena lives near Delhi, India, and attends school at night since she must stay at home during the day to babysit for her younger sister and do chores while her parents work.

Figure 4.6	Teaching Idea: The Institution of School: K-W-L Chart (Grades 1–3)

The study of school around the world lends itself well to the development of a K-W-L chart. Before sharing *A School Like Mine* (Smith & Shalev, 2007), the teacher could lead the children in discussing what they *know* about school and record their responses in the K column on the chart. After sharing the book, children could indicate *what* (in the W column) they would still like to know about schools in other parts of the world. At the conclusion of the study, the children could indicate what they have *learned* (in the L column) about the institution of school. In addition to writing their responses on the chart, children could also share what they have learned in various ways such as through art projects, drama, or writing.

This book can be paired with *My School in the Rain Forest: How Children Attend School Around the World*, by Canadian author Margriet Ruurs (2009). Twelve countries are featured in this book with some factual information about each such as the capital city, population, and official languages. The book's title refers to a school in the Guatemala rain forest. If children do not live in the village, they must take a boat on the Rio Dulce river to reach the school. Young children can independently read a book from the United Kingdom, *School Days Around the World* (Chambers, 2007), featuring children in Australia, Japan, India, Ghana, England, Peru, and United States. Samantha, in the United States, talks about her class's involvement in The Flat Stanley Project, begun by a teacher in Canada in 1995, which encourages letter writing among children across the globe. The project derives its title from the book *Flat Stanley* (Brown, 1964) whose original version was illustrated by the French illustrator Tomi Ungerer, recipient of the Hans Christian Andersen Award. You can learn how your class can become part of this project by consulting the website: www.flatstanley.com/.

After students have begun to compare and contrast schools in other parts of the world, they can read in more depth about school life in particular locations of interest and how it affects children and reflects the culture in which it is located. For example, the Indian residential schools of Canada are the focus of two books by Nicola I. Campbell (2005, 2008). The first one, *Shi-shi-etko* (2005), is about a little girl who knows that in four days she will be taken from her home by the Canadian government to attend Indian Residential School where she will lose her name and be forced to speak English. The sequel, *Shin-chi's Canoe* (2008) takes place the following year as Shi-shi-etko is about to return to school for the second year along with her little brother, Shin-Chi. Arriving at the school, Shi-shi-etko gives Shin-Chi a tiny cedar canoe their father has made, a little piece of their faraway home that he must keep hidden. In primary classrooms, teachers may want to provide a brief historical context to the book's setting. The book also portrays the resilience of childhood and how thoughts of those one loves can bring hope.

Like Shi-shi-etko and Shin-chi, Garmann is scared to start school in the translated picture book from Norway, *Garmann's Summer* (Hole, 2008) that received the BolognaRagazzi Award in 2007. The universal emotion of being fearful about a new experience is explored as Garmann's three great-aunts come to visit at the end of the summer and talk about all the things that frighten them. Garmann realizes that adults, as well as children, have fears. In *Listen to the Wind* (Mortenson & Roth, 2009), young readers are transported to the mountains of Pakistan. This informational picture book tells how Dr. Greg Mortenson helped the inhabitants of the village of Korphe build their own school. Readers learn that "Before our school was built, we had lessons outside. We wrote with sticks, on the ground." U.S. children also learn about the Pennies for Peace project and how they can help build schools in Pakistan and Afghanistan for children without any schools (see www.penniesforpeace.org).

Through global books, primary children can study in depth the concept of school and its diverse meanings. They will come to understand the integral role the institution of school plays in the lives of children around the world. In the next section, we present a genre study and explore how biographies and memoirs can support many of the social studies curriculum strands.

Biographies and Memoirs

(Upper Elementary/Middle School)

Children enjoy reading about the lives of real people as they satisfy a developmental need to imagine possibilities for their own lives. Many biographies and memoirs not only describe an individual's life but also provide insight into a historical time period or specific culture. As Zarnowski (2003) points out,

> Anyone who reads a biography learns about the time and place in which the subject lived—the larger social, political, and economic factors of the time. Biographies raise questions that affect the larger society—issues of war and peace, change, citizenship, human rights, use of resources and technology, and more. (p. 5)

In recent years, several memoirs have been written by adults who were children during China's cultural revolution, the decade (1966–1976) in the People's Republic of China during which the four olds—old ideas, old culture, old customs, and old habits—needed to be eliminated. Students can read both a male and female perspective on this historical time period. In *Red Scarf Girl: A Memoir of the Cultural Revolution*, by Ji-li Jiang (1997), the author describes how her happy life changed when she was 12 years old at the start of the Cultural Revolution. Da Chen (2001), who was only four when the Cultural Revolution began, also chronicles his childhood during this turbulent time in *China's Son: Growing Up in the Cultural Revolution*. The experiences of these two people can be compared and discussed. Both authors have webpages where students can find out more information about them today: www.jilijiang.com and www.dachen.org. These biographies link well to a study of China, its history, and contemporary society.

The civil war that ensued with the collapse of Yugoslavia is the context for *Zlata's Diary: A Child's Life in Sarajevo* (Filipovic, 1994). Zlata was 11 years old when the Bosnian war came to her beloved city of Sarajevo. In diary format from September 1991 through October 1993, Zlata records her thoughts and observations in real time as they are occurring, which makes this book especially appealing and immediate to young readers. Another memoir in diary form, *Thura's Diary: My Life in Wartime Iraq* (al-Windawi, 2004), was penned by 19-year-old Thura beginning on March 15, 2003, a week before the United States began bombing Iraq, and concluding June 4, 2003. An afterword and a postscript dated December 14, 2003, describe the capture of Saddam Hussein. This book could link to current events, help children understand the human side of U.S. actions, and prompt discussion on the United States' involvement in world conflicts. Both of these books provide a solid model for students to write their own diary entries.

To date, the Middle East continues to dominate the news. In Ibtisam Barakat's (2007) poignant memoir, *Tasting the Sky*, she describes her childhood in Ramallah in the occupied West Bank following the 1967 Six-Day War. Barakat focuses less on politics of the occupation and more on the thoughts and feelings of a young person seeking freedom. In an interview with *The Nation* (Bennet, 2007), Barakat notes, "Both Palestinians and Israelis have suffered greatly and need a home, freedom, and safety" (pp. 3–4). This memoir pairs well with the nonfiction photo-essay, *Neve Shalom/Wahat-al-Salam: Oasis of Peace* (Dolphin, 1993) that describes the village in Israel where Jews and Palestinian Arabs of Israeli citizenship live together in peace and harmony. More information about this community can be found on its website: http://nswas.org.

These memoirs provide insights into the experiences of young people living in specific historic times and cultural contexts, enable readers to experience events from a highly personal perspective, and gain insights into the thoughts and feelings of others living in challenging situations. A genre study of biography and memoir supports the social studies strands of "Culture," "Time, Continuity, and Change," "People, Places, and Environments," "Individual Development and Identity," and "Global Connections." In the final section of this chapter, we describe the topic of seeking peace and justice, a fundamental goal of international literature.

Figure 4.7 Teaching Idea: Memoir Project (Grades 6+)

Students can select a memoir described in this chapter or another memoir written by a person who grew up in another country. After reading the memoir, students can complete a memoir project about the person and the cultural context in which the person lived and then share their project orally in class. Students may choose from these kinds of projects: work with a partner to write an interview so that one student is the subject of the memoir and the other is an interviewer; assume the role of the person, and write and deliver a monologue about the highlights of your life; create a PowerPoint presentation about the person to share.

Seeking Peace and Justice

(All Grades)

The social studies standards describe a global perspective as one that "involves viewing the world and its people with understanding and concern. This perspective develops a sense of responsibility for the needs of all people and a commitment to finding just and peaceful solutions to global problems" (NCSS, n.d., Introduction, para. 31).

A global perspective of justice and peace is perfectly reflected in the translated picture book from Germany, *When I Grow Up, I Will Win the Nobel Peace Prize* (Pin, 2006). In first person, a young boy expresses all the things he will do when he grows up to "create peace in the world and among all people." This book naturally leads to a further study of the Nobel Peace Prize and recipients of the award, such as Nelson Mandela, Mother Teresa, or Jean Henri Dunant. Another picture book for young children, originally published in Great Britain, is *Talk Peace* (Williams, 2005). The lyrical text lends itself to children reciting aloud or creating movement to accompany the words. For example, one two-page spread reads, "Understand foreign land. Take heart, take part, talk peace." Children can express what peace means to them.

A good nonfiction companion to these picture books is *Peaceful Heroes* (Winter, 2009), a picture book with brief biographical vignettes of "ordinary people doing their best to protect ordinary people from being killed—*without even using a weapon*" (p. 2). The collection includes people from the United States as well as from other parts of the world, such as Gandhi, from India (already described in Chapter 2); Corrie ten Boom, from Holland, who opened her house as a hiding place for Jews during World War II; and Abdul Ghaffar Khan, from Pakistan, who believed Islam "was a religion of peace" and "defended the rights of Pashtuns against the British colonizers" (p. 34).

The United Nations adopted 54 principles affirming the Rights of the Child in 1989. *For Every Child* (Castle, 2001), published in Great Britain in association with UNICEF, presents 14 of these rights. Each right is depicted by an international illustrator, such as Philippe Dumas from Switzerland, P. J. Lynch from Ireland, and Satoshi Kitamura from Japan. Students can choose one of the rights and write their interpretation of what it means to them. For instance, Right Number 28, "Teach us all to read and write and teach us well so we grow up to be the best we can at whatever we wish to do," could be linked to the theme discussed earlier in this chapter on the institution of schools around the globe.

Finally, award-winning British author-illustrator Michael Foreman (2009) offers a message of renewal and hope in a world of war in *A Child's Garden: A Story of Hope*, which shows a young boy living behind a barbed wire fence who nurtures a small plant struggling to survive amidst the rubble. The text on the book's last page, illustrated in colorful watercolors, states, "One day the fence will disappear forever; and we will be able to walk again into the hills." The book can prompt discussion of how one child can make a difference and symbolically do something to bring peace and hope to the world.

The commitment to peace and justice in our world is a basic goal of the social studies curriculum. Global literature can provide various perspectives on this goal as well as ways that children themselves can work toward this goal.

Figure 4.8 Teaching Idea: Text Set of Cross-cultural Friendships (Grades 4–6+)

The following books about cross-cultural friendships—all discussed in this text—could form a text set (with multiple copies) in an upper elementary or middle school classroom: *The Storyteller's Beads* (Kurtz,1998), *Samir and Yonatan* (Carmi, 2000), *Burn My Heart* (Naidoo, 2007), *The Mzungu Boy* (Mwangi, 2005), *Number the Stars* (Lowry, 1989). The teacher could introduce these novels in a book talk to the class (see Lehman, 2007 for a sample book talk), and then students could sign up to read one of the books in a literature group. These small groups would meet to discuss their book. Then groups could share and compare what they learned about cross-cultural friendships. The class could develop a matrix chart to record these comparisons.

Conclusion

This chapter presents many opportunities for global literature to support the social studies standards. We have discussed a wide variety of books and described ways they can be incorporated into the social studies curriculum. The next chapter turns our attention to global literature for science and mathematics.

5

Science and Mathematics

Aesop's fables, a part of our world literary heritage, provide the inspiration for Stephanie Gwyn Brown's (2003) *Professor Aesop's the Crow and the Pitcher*. This updated twist cleverly portrays a crow employing the scientific method to solve the problem of satisfying his urgent thirst. In the process, he uses mathematics to measure the pebbles he drops in the pitcher, the water level, and his levels of determination, thirst, and the ambient temperature. In the end, he shows himself to be a "true scientist" by communicating the procedures and results of his successful experiment.

Children's Literature and STEM Education

That ancient fable appropriately introduces our discussion in this chapter on the ways that international books can be incorporated in science and mathematics instruction. As a framework, we use the national context of science, technology, engineering, and mathematics (STEM) education. STEM is the term currently favored to highlight the importance of these four areas in advancing American economic and technological global leadership (STEM, n.d.). In response to a projected shortage of scientists and engineers in the future workforce, STEM education seeks to promote careers in these areas and to attract students to these disciplines. Its key principles, as identified by Janice S. Morrison (2006) in a monograph on the Teaching Institute for Essential Science website, are problem solving, innovation, invention, self-reliance, logical thinking, technological literacy, and cultural relevance.

Furthermore, STEM education, according to Morrison (2006), is "trans-disciplinary," with technology and engineering embedded in mathematics and science courses (p. 4). This view suggests an integration of these disciplines, and we believe that literature can play an important role in integrating content across these subjects, as across all others. We also believe that literature is highly compatible with STEM principles, cited above, while attracting students' interest in STEM topics. Also, by including global books, we can demonstrate the cultural diversity and relevance of these subjects to our students. For example, in *The Number Devil*, Hans Magnus Enzensberger (1997) employs wit and trickery to engage young readers in an adventurous fantasy while learning solid mathematical principles, all enlivened by Rotraut Susanne Berner's droll illustrations. This book, originally published in Germany, pairs well with Jon Scieszka's (1995) *Math Curse*, which similarly portrays how the qualities of mathematics that so bedevil some learners can be viewed humorously.

Literature also promotes integration with other subject areas, such as language arts. For example, literature helps readers to grasp the significance of science encountered in some books, especially science fiction and fantasy. British author Philip Pullman's (2005) *His Dark Materials* trilogy (*The Golden Compass, The Subtle Knife,* and *The Amber Spyglass,* all republished with new material) has achieved international acclaim. Now there is a companion text, *The Science of Philip Pullman's His Dark Materials,* by Mary and John Gribbin (2005), that explains the science behind the books. Likewise, in Nancy Farmer's (2002) *The House of the Scorpion*, set in a futuristic country called Opium wedged between the United States and Mexico, the controversial issue of human cloning plays a central role in the plot. Farmer acknowledges that she draws upon current events and scientific issues, like cloning, as inspiration for her award-winning fiction (Vardell, 2004). These kinds of titles provide exciting connections with science and technology and related ethical dilemmas.

Figure 5.1   Profile: Philip Pullman

Best known for *His Dark Materials* fantasy series, Philip Pullman was born in Norwich, England in the fall of 1946. As a child, he and his brother spent a lot of time with their grandfather, an Anglican priest, who loved to tell his grandsons stories (Miller, 2005). Pullman spent his youth living in England, Australia, Zimbabwe, and North Wales (Pullman, 2009). His father died in a plane crash when Pullman was seven, and after his mother remarried, Pullman enjoyed a large family of step and half siblings (Miller, 2005).

Pullman studied English at Exeter College in Oxford, where he remained. Upon finishing his degree, he taught literature to middle school students. He married his wife, Jude, and had two sons before deciding to focus on his writing. He has maintained his passion for education, believing his enthusiasm has, at times, led him to "make foolish and ill-considered remarks alleging that not everything is well in our schools. [His] main concern is that an over-emphasis on testing and league tables [sports comparison charts] has led to a lack of time and freedom for a true, imaginative and humane engagement with literature" (Pullman, 2009). He has also asserted that when it comes to having students engage with poetry, he preferred to have students read aloud to experience the poem more vividly (Pullman, 2005).

A humanist and atheist, Pullman has been critiqued for how he portrays Christianity in his successful and well-honored *His Dark Materials* series: *The Golden Compass* (1996) (which was made into a movie in 2008), *The Subtle Knife* (1997), *The Amber Spyglass* (2000), and shorter companion books: *Lyra's Oxford* (2003), *Once Upon a Time in the North* (2008) and forthcoming, *The Book of Dust*. Pullman admits that reading John Milton's *Paradise Lost* aloud as a student helped inspire the atmosphere he wanted to create in the series (Pullman, 2005).

Many of Pullman's novels include strong female characters: His first children's book, a middle grade historical suspense novel, *Count Karlstein* (1982), and his other major historical young adult series featuring Sally Lockhart, a female detective in Victorian England (*The Ruby in the Smoke*, 1985, *The Shadow in the North*, 1988, *The Tiger in the Well*, 1990, and *The Tin Princess* 1994).

For younger readers, he has several stories that he describes as "fairy tales" (Pullman, 2009), which tend to be stand-alone novels that include fairy tale and folkloric dimensions. Among these titles are: *I Was a Rat!* (1999), *Clockwork: Or All Wound Up* (1998), and *The Scarecrow and His Servant* (2004). Pullman admits he finds these types of stories "very enjoyable" to read but also very "difficult to write" (Pullman, 2009).

The products of Pullman's many years of writing have earned him a British Book Award, the Guardian Children's Fiction Award, a Carnegie Medal, and the Whitbread Book Award, among others. His books are often concerned with the tensions between economic classes, the past and present, childhood and adulthood, good and evil, and many other themes central to the human experience.

—M. D. Julian-Kessel

In today's world, there are plenty of problems—ethical and otherwise—to solve, so the STEM goal of problem solving will have ample opportunities for application. Global literature can raise awareness of important problems and stimulate action in response. Books can provide meaningful contexts for and demonstrations of the scientific processes of inquiry, observation, prediction, and inference, as well as the use of mathematical reasoning and logic to measure observations, analyze data, examine patterns and relationships, and solve problems. Students will learn new terms and use language to communicate findings orally and in writing. The remainder of this chapter is organized around selected topics, or themes, relevant to STEM education. We suggest possible international book titles and practices that can address national science and math standards.

Animals: Other Creatures That Share Our Earth

We begin with a topic that interests most young readers: the nonhuman beings that inhabit the world. Of this vast animal diversity, we present a few that are represented in high-quality recent global titles. These books, in turn, can be springboards for connections to many other examples that teachers may already know. For example, *Sea Horse: The Shyest Fish in the Sea,* by English author Chris Butterworth (2006), introduces children to the life cycle and activities of this unusual fish, along with the scientific names of different sea horse types. Readers may want to learn more about its coral habitat and will soon discover the precarious state of many of the earth's reefs. Online inquiries will lead to the National Oceanic and Atmospheric Administration's coral reef conservation program (coralreef.noaa.gov/) or the Coral Reef Alliance (www.coral.org/), an international organization working to preserve endangered reefs. This is a good means to introduce three other topics we discuss later: conservation, habitats, and life cycles. It also may be a good way to initiate social action in response to problem solving.

Dr. Paula Kahumbu and photographer Peter Greste, both from Kenya, have teamed with various American authors to tell true stories about African animals that will enthrall children and offer opportunities for curriculum connections. In the pair of books, *Owen & Mzee: The True Story of a Remarkable Friendship* (Hatkoff, Hatkoff, & Kahumbu, 2006) and *Owen & Mzee: The Language of Friendship* (Hatkoff, Hatkoff, & Kahumbu, 2007), children meet the baby hippo Owen who was orphaned in the 2004 tsunami, rescued, and taken to the Kenyan animal sanctuary, Haller Park. Here, Owen adopted Mzee, a very old Aldabra tortoise, as his mother. Color photographs bring Owen and Mzee's story to life for children who will be curious to learn more about the Aldabra tortoise and animal sanctuaries. They can also further investigate tsunamis—their causes, effects, and locations—and how the 2004 tsunami affected people by reading *Tsunami: Helping Each Other* (Morris & Larson, 2005) that describes how two brothers, aged 8 and 12, survived this tragedy.

Figure 5.2	Teaching Idea: Tsunami Study: A Math Connection (Grades 4–6+)

After reading the two books about Owen and Mzee (Hatkoff, Hatkoff, & Kahumbu, 2006, 2007) and *Tsunami: Helping Each Other* (Morris & Larson, 2005) and then investigating tsunamis, students can further explore mathematical connections in several ways. For example, they can graph information about tsunamis, both past and present, including wave height and wave length. The students can learn about the Pacific Tsunami Warning System and the computer models that predict the arrival of a tsunami within minutes. They can also determine the years when the most well-known tsunamis occurred and calculate the number of years between them to look for patterns.

British author Nick Dowson (2007) transports readers to the mountains of China to learn about the panda bear in *Tracks of a Panda*. Children learn about the importance of bamboo as a food source for the panda and how their black and white fur provides camouflage in the winter. Teachers could bring in bamboo to show the children, allowing them to feel it and describe its properties. The book provides a good introduction to the concept of camouflage, leading to a discussion of other animals that use camouflage to survive.

Another British author, Martin Jenkins (2007), a conservation biologist, introduces children to the five kinds of great apes in *Ape*. Children learn about the orangutan, chimp, bonobo, and gorilla. They then find out that "the fifth kind of great ape is . . . do you know who? You . . . me." A map at the end of the book enables children to compare the habitats of the four apes and see how many of each species remain. Children are exposed to new vocabulary terms—such as *durian*, a fruit in Southeast Asia eaten by orangutans—in a meaningful context. The book provides an appropriate way to introduce the concept of evolution to children.

Building on children's natural interest in and curiosity about animals may be a good way to introduce the richness and diversity of the world beyond our borders. Many of the most interesting, unique animals exist only (outside of zoos) in other countries, so learning about them presents the perfect link to study those regions.

Life Cycles and Other Patterns

The life cycles of animals and plants form one of the most common patterns in nature, and noting such regularities is part of mathematical reasoning. Jonathan London (2001) poetically portrays the importance of the annual rain cycle for both animal and human life on the East African savanna in *What the Animals Were Waiting For*. Readers can envision the Maasai people's dependence on rain for the new grass that feeds both domestic and wild animals. Although not depicted in this book, when rains do not arrive—sometimes for years—leading to severe drought, people and animals can suffer famine and starvation. This is another topic that invites further inquiry and potential problem solving. Students also could compare annual rainfall averages between their region and the savanna of Kenya and Tanzania in East Africa.

The photo-essay, *Cycle of Rice, Cycle of Life*, by Jan Reynolds (2009), captures the rhythm and interconnectivity of the water cycle and growing rice in Bali, Indonesia. The traditional method of sustainable farming is disrupted by a government policy for continuous rice planting that ignored the old environmentally responsible model. The author relates this mistaken policy to food wastefulness in the United States and proposes solutions that students and teachers could explore, such as learning where our food originates, growing and buying more food locally, and composting.

One Child, One Seed, by Kathryn Cave (2002) from England, set in rural South Africa, demonstrates a simple numerical pattern of counting from 1 to 10 and one-to-one correspondence. Each page depicts the concept of a particular number in four ways, and a complete chart at the end displays the 10 numbers graphically. A pumpkin's life cycle and children's daily homestead activities also are portrayed in South African photographer Gisèle Wulfsohn's pictures and Cave's informative text. American students can compare and contrast pumpkins raised in South Africa and North America and the different ways they are prepared to be eaten. Simple math and science processes would be employed to make the dish of *isijingi* described in the recipe included at the end.

Demi's (1997) *One Grain of Rice* demonstrates a different kind of pattern: mathematical exponents. In this folktale from India, a peasant girl cleverly outwits a selfish raja who refuses to share rice with his famished subjects. Her plan to teach him a lesson involves doubling one grain of rice each day for 30 days. Much to the raja's surprise, this accumulates to more than one billion grains, and a chart at the end displays the totals for all the days. This story vividly dramatizes an intriguing mathematical concept and could inspire students to compose original tales like this about other math concepts, such as numbers and operations, geometry, and measurement. They could develop charts, graphs, or other ways to represent these ideas and principles.

Patterns, including life cycles, can be found everywhere in natural and man-made environments, and we can encourage our students to find good examples as a way to promote mathematical thinking.

Stephen Swinburne's (1998) *Lots and Lots of Zebra Stripes* does just this with colorful photographs, and a study of such patterns in nature can lead to investigating their variety in locations across the globe.

Habitats Around the World

Studies of animals and life cycles involve learning about different habitats, which can help children to develop a sense of the world (a science concept) and spatial understanding. British author Sean Taylor's (2008) *The Great Snake* uses his actual trip up the Amazon River in Brazil as the premise for a collection of stories that he gathers along the way. Interspersed with the stories are his descriptions of the river, its surrounding rain forest and animal life, and its climate. Taylor includes the impact of this habitat on human life and discusses the destruction of the rainforest, citing an organization that works for sustainable development in the Amazon. Students could investigate what effect the loss of rainforests has on our lives and research more about this and other organizations to find out what Americans can do to help solve the problem.

Young children gain an initial understanding of the forest as a kind of habitat in a book from France, *In the Forest*, illustrated by Pierre de Hugo, by Danielle Denega (2002). Designed with foldouts, children open the flaps to learn about plants and animals that live in the forest. At the end of the book, a double-page spread identifies forest trees and invites children to recognize the trees by their leaves and fruits. Teachers can share samples of these leaves and fruits and encourage children to find their own samples in the local community to create a display with labels and brief descriptions in the classroom.

British zoologist Nicola Davies (2006) describes habitats with "extreme" climates in *Extreme Animals: The Toughest Creatures on Earth*. This humorous book takes children to both poles, the desert, the ocean depths, and even inside volcanoes to learn about these habitats and their animals. Scientific vocabulary and concepts are introduced in this book, such as *magma, black smokers, cells, cold-blooded,* and *warm-blooded*. Children can generate a chart of living things that are cold- and warm-blooded or that compares the habitats described in the book. Children can engage in experiments to demonstrate the difference between extreme heat and cold.

As children learn about a topic of high interest to them—animals and where they live—they also should recognize the precarious state of many animals' natural homes. Animal habitats are often affected by humans, who exert the greatest impact on environmental change, a topic we investigate next.

Environmental Change
and the Need for Conservation

Whether it is shrinking rainforests, expanding desert, rising oceans, increased river flooding, more severe storms such as hurricanes, or warmer temperatures—all these situations are due to climate change, much of it because of human activity. Therefore, we bear great responsibility to understand the problems and take actions to solve or lessen them. We also need to understand how interconnected and interdependent the earth's systems, habitats, and organisms are. What happens on the opposite side of the globe affects us and vice versa.

Wangari Maathai is a Kenyan woman who decided to make a difference in response to the deforestation that was creating erosion and expanding the desert in her homeland. A highly educated environmentalist, she started the Green Belt Movement in Kenya in 1977 and won the Nobel Peace Prize in 2004 for her work, which by then had spread to 30 African countries and resulted in the planting of 30 million trees across the continent. (To find out more about this organization, the woman who founded it, and how to get involved, visit the website www.greenbeltmovement.org/.) The simple text and brilliant acrylic paintings of Jeanette Winter's *Wangari's Trees of Peace* (2008) present this true story that may inspire young environmentalists to observe what is happening to trees in their own communities. Are trees being removed to make way for new buildings? Are abandoned buildings and parking lots allowed to become eyesores, and could they be replaced with trees? Are new trees planted when dead or diseased trees are cut down in neighborhoods? These questions could prompt first-hand research, data gathering, and possibly motivation for action.

Fernando's Gift/El regalo de Fernando (Keister, 1995) is an informational text that presents efforts to preserve Costa Rica's rain forest, enhanced with full-color photographs. Fernando's story, in which he takes action to replant trees and to save ones already there, is presented in parallel English and Spanish text. For current information about the Children's Eternal Rainforest in Costa Rica, visit www.acmcr.org/home.htm. As a follow-up, a class could launch meaningful science projects related to tropical biomes and conservation and use math to devise ways to earn money to support environmental efforts.

The Sherpas of Tibet and Nepal are best known for their expert guidance to climbers of Mount Everest. Since 1976, however, with the establishment of Sagarmatha National Park on the upper part of the mountain, Sherpas also work as park rangers and guardians of forest use and wildlife protection. In *Sacred Mountain Everest*, Christine Taylor-Butler (2009), details their essential role and accomplishments, along with explanation of the mountain's formation, climate zones, and glaciers. The book ends with information about the American Himalayan Foundation (2006), an organization dedicated to "providing . . . education, health care, cultural and environmental preservation" (www.himalayan-foundation.org) for the region's people. Science classes could visit their website and learn more about their projects to protect the environment, how to get involved, and the Sherpas' contributions to this work.

Deforestation, caused by political unrest and the establishment of refugee camps near the mountains in the Democratic Republic of Congo, has threatened the natural habitat and depleted the population of the mountain gorilla. In *Looking for Miza* (Hatkoff, Hatkoff, Hatkoff, & Kahumbu, 2008), children visit the Virunga National Park, home to the endangered mountain gorillas. They meet two dedicated park rangers who patrol the park and guard against hunting and poaching, which although illegal, continues to exist in the park. Children can visit the blog of these park rangers (www.wildlife direct.org) and then assume the role of a park ranger, writing a blog entry about their day after they investigate more information about the mountain gorillas and identify other endangered animals. Students can create a chart listing the animals, where they live, and the reasons for their endangered status. If there are personnel from a local zoo or conservation organization who could visit the class, students could generate questions about gorillas and endangered species to ask the visitor.

Figure 5.3 Teaching Idea: Social Action Project (All Grades)

Many books in this chapter focus on endangered species or conservation of natural resources. After reading books and consulting related websites, students can participate in a social-action project. The class could collectively decide on the project's focus and what they will do. A few ideas include conducting a fund-raiser for one of the organizations, developing a public awareness campaign in the school and/or community, writing letters to legislatures to express their concern about the issue, and volunteering their time to assist a local nonprofit conservation agency or organization.

The health of our natural environment affects the whole planet, and in some ways, may be the single issue that most interconnects the world. We cannot afford to shrug off environmental problems as belonging to someone else. They also have an enormous effect on human health, which we explore in the next section.

World Health Awareness

Promoting good health and combating disease have always been global issues, but in today's ever-shrinking world, the consequences for not attending to them effectively can be devastating. Some problems, such as tuberculosis and HIV/AIDS, have been with us for centuries or decades; some, such as polio or smallpox, seem to have been nearly eradicated only to reappear; and some, like H1N1 ("swine") flu, are new strains of old foes. All of these, in addition to typical childhood illnesses, seriously affect the lives of young people around the world whether they contract the diseases themselves or their caregivers do.

Home Now, by South African author Lesley Beake (2007), depicts this situation when young Sieta loses her parents to AIDS, and she comes to live with Aunty in a strange place. This fictional picture book is a good way to introduce the topic to young children, who will readily understand the plight of losing parents. According to Canadian author Deborah Ellis's (2005) *Our Stories, Our Songs*, "AIDS . . . has orphaned 11.5 million children in Sub-Saharan Africa. The number is expected to rise to 20 million by the year 2020" (p. vii). This book gathers stories from children in Zambia and Malawi whose lives have been touched by HIV/AIDS, along with additional factual material and suggested resources for books and organizations.

Two other novels present the lives of older children who are orphaned because of AIDS: *The Heaven Shop*, also by Deborah Ellis (2004), set in Malawi, and fellow Canadian Allan Stratton's (2004) *Chanda's Secrets*, set in an unnamed southern African country. In addition to coping with survival themselves, both Binti and Chanda, the protagonists, must devise ways of staying or reuniting with their siblings. In Chanda's case, the children also must face the question of their own HIV status.

Indeed, children sometimes are infected by their mothers in childbirth, and the problem of HIV/AIDS is not restricted to Africa. In *Ana's Story*, Jenna Bush (2008), who interned with UNICEF in South America, recounts the experiences of such a teenager. Both Ana's and Chanda's stories also illustrate the additional devastating effects on young people's lives of shame, misunderstanding, and secrecy regarding the disease. These books can initiate critical discussions about the importance of honesty and openness in seeking diagnosis and treatment, as well as practicing prevention.

HIV is just one example of a worldwide health issue, and new ones appear each year. Worldwide epidemics are ancient, with the 14th-century Black Plague perhaps one of the most infamous. James Cross Giblin's (1995) *When Plague Strikes: The Black Death, Smallpox, AIDS* places today's crises in a historical context and is a book worth revisiting with older students. Other more mundane, but nevertheless critical, problems, such as securing clean drinking water or providing adequate health care, require proficient scientific, technological, and engineering skills and thinking.

Technology: The Benefits, Risks, Costs, and Ethical Issues

Sandwiched between the disciplines of science and mathematics in STEM education, technology (along with engineering, which is addressed in the next section) is a tool to be used in both the generation and application of scientific and mathematical knowledge. One of the goals for STEM is that students will recognize these interconnections, appreciate the benefits, risks, and costs of technology, and grapple with the ensuing ethical issues and global challenges.

The United States' development and use of the atom bomb was perhaps the most graphic example of such a technological dilemma. While the bomb's use ended World War II, it did so at enormous human and physical cost and had consequences that still haunt us today. In *Hiroshima: The Story of the First Atom Bomb*, British author Clive A. Lawton (2004) discusses the history and science of the bomb's development and devastating aftermath for survivors' health. In a section on "Was It the Right Decision?" the author presents different perspectives but also explains how using the bomb actually postponed world peace and created a dangerous new situation that still exists for the world. The human face of this challenge is poignantly depicted in *Shin's Tricycle* by Tatsuharu Kodama (1995). In August 1945, Shin had just received a red tricycle for his fourth birthday when the atom bomb was dropped on Hiroshima, killing the young boy, his two older sisters, and his best friend, Kimi. When Shin's father discovered the tricycle buried in the backyard, he donated it to the Peace Museum in Hirohsima, where it is displayed as a reminder of the destructive power of technology.

However, as noted earlier, in *Cycle of Rice, Cycle of Life*, by Jan Reynolds (2009), American scientists were able to use computer technology to help them make a case to the Indonesian government for returning to sustainable rice farming methods. The computer model these scientists developed now assists the traditional prediction and decision making of farmers and priests, and similar models help to promote environmentally friendly farming practices in other places around the globe.

By considering these and other examples of technology's tragic outcomes and positive benefits, students and teachers can study ways to minimize the bad and maximize the good and to recognize that some consequences cannot be anticipated. Science teaching needs to examine the potential conflicts posed by and the limitations of technology. Books can remind us of the ethics of technology not only for ourselves but also for others around the world.

Figure 5.4	Classroom Vignette: International Literature Bags (Grades 1–2)

In 2008, my coteachers and I began using literature bags to support student learning. These canvas bags contain two to four books (fiction and nonfiction) on a topic and a writing journal. The books vary in text difficulty to provide diverse learners an opportunity to independently read or hear the story read by a family member. The bags have a small index card fastened to the handle with a list of the materials inside and ideas for writing activities to do after reading.

To create literature bags, first, decide the topic and begin a book search. Then, purchase one canvas bag and one journal per book set. Invite your parents to decorate the bags—a great way to build community and a quick way to assemble the bags. Finally, develop several journal options for children to complete after they read. On an index card, list the materials in the bag and the journal options. Place the contents in the bag, and attach the card to the handle.

When I noticed that books about cultural practices of people on the different continents were missing, I started making global children's literature bags. For example, the Transportation bag contributes to many academic content standards from my state: comparing forms of transportation past and present; describing the cultural practices and products of people on different continents; explaining why people in different parts of the world earn a living in a variety of ways; and recognizing that money is a generally accepted medium of exchange for goods and services and that different countries use different forms of money. Books included in this set are *Tap-Tap* by Karen Lynn Williams (1994), set in Haiti; *Bikes for Rent!* by Isaac Olaleye (2001), set in Nigeria; and *This Boat* and *This Car*, both by Paul Collicutt (2001, 2002), showing boats and cars from around the world. Journal options include a formal letter to a character, a Venn diagram for readers to compare themselves to the characters, an investigation of countries, and creating illustrations and descriptions of students' favorite vehicles.

(Continued)

(Continued)

> A second international bag is folktales from around the world. The international titles for this set include *Nabulela* (Moodie, 1996), set in South Africa; *Clever Ali* (Farmer, 2006), set in Egypt; and *Goha the Wise Fool* (Johnson-Davies, 2005), set in the Middle East. Journal options for this set include a Venn diagram comparing two of the stories, a web that shows important events from one story, and an informal letter describing favorite things from a story.
>
> The students in my classroom are assigned one literature bag per week. They go home on Thursday and are returned on Tuesday. Students read at least one book and complete one journal activity. Feedback from a parent survey was overwhelmingly positive about the content of the bags and the assignments. The children show their enthusiasm each week as they race into the classroom in anticipation to see which bag they will get next.
>
> *Teacher: Angela Johnson Rietschlin, Grade 2, Galena, Ohio*

How Things Are Made and How They Work

The E in STEM refers to engineering, a wide-ranging field that may not be well known to children, but tangible evidence of engineering surrounds us. Engineering involves the application of scientific and mathematical principles to solve practical problems. Engineers design aircraft, roads, railways, bridges, and buildings. They are inventors, they help us see how things work, and they figure out how to heat and cool buildings.

British science author Neil Ardley has partnered with author-illustrator David Macaulay (1998) to provide a fascinating and comprehensive book on engineering. The subtitle of *The New Way Things Work, From Lever to Lasers, Windmills to Websites: A Visual Guide to the World of Machines,* invites readers to investigate such common objects as a can opener, hand drill, and sewing machine. Limitless possibilities present themselves for hands-on activities, experiments, and constructing projects. Teachers may want to invite an engineer to class to discuss her work and conduct demonstrations or arrange a field trip to a local manufacturer to observe how a product is made.

Shortlisted for the Royal Society Prize for Junior Science in the United Kingdom, *How Nearly Everything Was Invented* (MacLeod, 2006) describes various inventions. A group of cartoon characters, called The Brainwaves, guide children on this international adventure of discovery. In small groups, students could conceptualize and create their own inventions and share these with children in other classrooms. Many cities sponsor "Invention Conventions" which would provide students another venue for displaying their creations.

Two children's books give students a glimpse into how the work of engineers is applied around the globe. A truly international book is *Super Structures: Inside the World's Most Spectacular Buildings* (Bos, 2008) with an Australian author, British consultant, and Italian illustrators. Readers tour the globe to learn about the "building blocks" of all kinds of structures like the Diocletian's Palace in Croatia and the Millau Viaduct in France. *Great Building Stories of the Past* (Kent, 2001) describes methods used to build such structures as the Great Pyramid, the Great Wall of China, and the Eiffel Tower. Detailed illustrations and diagrams provide insight into the construction process. Children could choose one of the structures described in these books to investigate further. They could construct their own model of the structure and explain to classmates the steps they took. Teachers could share videos and websites about these structures with the class. If any students have visited one of these sites, they could share impressions and photos with classmates.

Engineering, with its emphasis on designing and building many kinds of physical things, appeals naturally to children's interests in manipulating concrete items. Books such as these can extend their ability to explore and understand how things are built and work—skills that may help them possibly invent new tools and design solutions to future problems.

Figure 5.5 Teaching Idea: Invention Cards (Grades 4–6+)

Students could select an invention mentioned in one of the books in this chapter to create an invention card. The cards would include the name of the invention, who invented it, when and where it was invented, and how the invention has helped people, animals, or society. Students should draw a picture of the invention or find a picture of it to attach to the cards. The main parts of the invention should be labeled. (See Robb, 2003, p. 334, for a sample). These cards can be used in a variety of ways. Students can share them with younger students, develop a class file of these inventions for students to share among themselves, use them as a basis for an invention center in the classroom, or create an "Invention Museum" in the school's hall or library.

Scientific and Mathematical Contributions From Diverse Cultures

In the United States, we often laud our national scientific and mathematical accomplishments, but one of the most important ideas we can teach our children is that such talent is global, and that we benefit from recognizing and learning knowledge developed in other cultures. For example, when students study algebra, how many of them learn that ninth-century Persian scholars devised the name *algebra* and the term *algorithm*? Do children study the origins of zero—in ancient Babylon (now Iraq) and the Maya of Mexico? Teachers may be familiar with David Schwartz's (1998) math alphabet book, *G Is for Googol*, a whimsical compendium of math history and terms with fascinating information, such as the invention of the abacus (a type of calculator) in China, the Italian Fibonacci (whom we can thank for our use of Arabic numerals—which, of course, were invented by Arabs—instead of the more difficult Roman variety), and the West African mathematical reasoning board game of oware. Although many of the descriptions do not include the concepts' origins, this source provides a potentially fruitful supply of ideas for further investigation about global connections.

In biographies, children meet scientists and mathematicians from around the globe who have made significant contributions. One focus of many STEM initiatives is the encouragement of girls to enter the STEM fields. Learning about women who have contributed to these areas can provide positive role models for girls and can inform all children that STEM fields are not for boys only. In the primary grades, teachers can share D. Anne Love's (2006) picture-book biography, *Of Numbers and Stars: The Story of Hypatia*, who lived in Alexandria, Egypt, and is considered the first woman mathematician. Children can locate Alexandria on the globe and learn more about this important city in ancient times. They can discuss the author's note that indicates the challenges of locating information about Hypatia and connect the search for information to science and mathematical investigation.

Older children will be inspired by the life of Marie Curie, the Polish chemist who was the first woman to receive the Nobel Prize not just once, but twice. *Something Out of Nothing: Marie Curie and Radium*, by Carla Killough McClafferty (2006), chronicles the remarkable story of her life. Students can learn more about radium and why this discovery was such an important one. They can find out more about the Nobel Prize in the sciences (physics, chemistry, physiology, or medicine) to identify other women who have received this coveted honor.

Like Hypatia, Galileo Galilei also was interested in the stars, as depicted in Peter Sís's (1996) *Starry Messenger*, an account of the work of the famous Italian mathematician, astronomer, and physicist. In the 16th and 17th centuries, it was heresy to challenge the conventional view of the earth as the center of the universe, but Galileo did just that when he published the record of his starry observations as viewed through his telescope. (For an overview of scientific thinking in this period, see

Anno's Medieval World, by the Hans Christian Andersen Award-winning Japanese author-illustrator Mitsumasa Anno, 1979.) Sis's picture book vividly demonstrates the power of careful observation and communication of scientific findings, as his work ultimately transformed humankind's view of the world. This biography provides a wonderful introduction to the study of the solar system and to a discussion (which could be enhanced with a visit to a planetarium) of how our knowledge of astronomy continues to be refined as new discoveries are made.

From the starry heavens to the sea's depths, Dan Yaccarino (2009) portrays *The Fantastic Undersea Life of Jacques Cousteau*. This 20th-century French scientist, who invented diving equipment and assembled a research team for deep sea exploration, developed waterproof cameras to record his observations and used these to create an award-winning film and two well-known television series. He also became an advocate for environmental preservation and founded the Cousteau Society, which has joined with UNESCO to form an interdisciplinary education and research program. A prominent group of scientists in this program hold endowed chairs at universities around the world. Science classes can learn more about their work on the website www.cousteau.org and find links to YouTube videos of Cousteau.

People throughout history and across the globe have contributed knowledge to the STEM fields. By reading about these scientists and mathematicians, children gain an awareness of how our lives in the United States have been directly influenced by people and cultures of the world.

Earning, Saving, and Investing Money

Children around the world can relate to the idea of earning and saving money to buy something they dearly want, and more-privileged children can learn how much harder that can be for those who have much less materially. From three different regions—Central America and East and West Africa—three boys work and save their earnings to get a bicycle.

In *Pedrito's Day*, by Nicaragua native Luis Garay (1997), a young boy shines shoes to earn three coins at a time for a bicycle that he can use to help Mama carry their loads of tortillas and tamales to market. Similarly, in Tololwa M. Mollel's (1999) *My Rows and Piles of Coins* set in Tanzania, Saruni stacks the coins he saves in piles and arranges the piles in rows to count the 30 shillings and 50 cents it takes to buy a bicycle. An author's note explains how many shillings equal one dollar. Students could calculate the cost of Saruni's bike in American dollars and compare that to the current value of a new bicycle. In author Isaac Olaleye's (2001) native Nigeria, Lateef yearns to rent a bike and saves the money he earns by selling mushrooms, firewood, and learning how to repair bikes, as portrayed in *Bikes for Rent!* Realizing one's dreams by setting goals and overcoming setbacks are important themes in all three books, which help children realize the value of money and saving to accomplish their desires.

Figure 5.6	Profile: Tololwa Mollel

Tololwa Mollel, born in the Arusha region of Tanzania, is known for recreating African tribal tales and producing original stories. Mollel hopes his stories will educate children about different cultural backgrounds as well as focusing on customary morals and values. In 1991, Mollel published *The Orphan Boy,* his first major book. Within a year of being published, *The Orphan Boy* earned the Amelia Howard-Gibbon Award, the Governor General's Award, the Elizabeth Cleaver Award, and the Parents' Choice Storybook Award, and appeared on the Canadian Library Association and American Booksellers Association's notable book lists.

Throughout the 1990s, Mollel wrote and illustrated several children's books. Some, like *The Orphan Boy,* were spun from African tribal tales. Others, such as *My Rows and Piles of Coins* (1999), were tales that were based upon experiences in Mollel's life while growing up in East Africa. Mollel's goal is to write books that will teach and encourage each child to think, and he typically incorporates valuable themes within his books. One theme that is touched on repeatedly is that assumptions and reality are two different things, as in *Rhinos for Lunch and Elephants for Supper!* (1991). Another theme that is carried over in many of Mollel's books is the value of logic and wit; by using logic and wit, you can challenge opinions and create change in the world. *The King and the Tortoise* (1993) and *Shadow Dance* (1998) are examples of works that articulate this theme.

Rhinos for Lunch and Elephants for Supper! is a retelling of a traditional tribal story, Mollel uses the trickster character to encourage understanding of the world and to prompt children to think. When Mollel became a well-known author, he moved away from telling tribal tales to writing books that reflected his childhood in Tanzania. Mollel realized that children were not being exposed to other cultures. He wanted to show what it was like to grow up in an oral culture that relied on extended family and the community (Zerbonia, 2010). Mollel's *Big Boy* (1995), *Kele's Secret* (1997), and *My Rows and Piles of Coins* are all books that reflect Mollel's childhood experiences in Tanzania.

Although Mollel continues to write children's stories, in 2000 he directed his attention to the theater. At various schools, Mollel helped students create plays for his books: *Subira, Subira* (2000*), Song Bird* (1999*),* and *A Promise to the Sun* (1992). In the summer of 2000, Mollel worked with the Children-In-Dance company in Calgary, Alberta, and produced *The Visit of the Sea Queen,* which received rave reviews. Mollel is now a citizen of Canada and lives in Edmonton, Alberta, with his family.

—*Autumn Reed*

Two more books—again from East and West Africa and both true stories—demonstrate the power of gifts or small loans put to good use. In *Beatrice's Goat*, Page McBrier (2001) recounts how a young girl and her family living in Uganda benefit from receiving a goat from Heifer International to eventually obtain an education and build a better house. The organization's website for educators (www.heifereducation.org) provides lesson plans and classroom activities, books and other multimedia resources, and ways to get involved and make a difference, such as raising money as a class project to contribute toward animals like Beatrice received.

The second book, Katie Smith Milway's (2008) *One Hen: How One Small Loan Made a Big Difference* presents the story of Kojo, whose village in Ghana loans him money to buy a chicken that sets in motion a series of events, eventually culminating in the idea of "village banks." These banks give small loans to people who can then start their own businesses, a concept that has grown into the global microfinance organization called Opportunity International (www.opportunity.org). The related website, www.onehen.org, provides lessons and teaching ideas on "microfinance for kids" and how to donate money. Both of these books encourage children to take action in ways that are within their reach.

Learning about currencies and finance involves mathematical skills, such as counting, converting between various currencies of the world, and executing operations with numbers. However, the books in this section regarding earning, saving, and investing money also offer good potential for connections with economics education, which links to social studies education.

Figure 5.7	Teaching Idea: Money Around the World (Grades 4–6)

Depending on their age level, students can work as a whole class, in small groups, with a partner, or individually to create a display or class book about money around the world. Students could research different kinds of currency in various countries and describe these monetary systems. A class book, with a page for each country's currency, could be compiled. Students could also develop a comparative chart showing the similarities and differences among the monetary systems. They could further determine current conversion rates between the dollar and other world currencies, compute various conversions, and write math story problems about the conversions.

Conclusion

Like satisfying one's physical thirst (as the crow did in *Professor Aesop*, Brown, 2003), children's literature can play an important role in satisfying thirst for knowledge in STEM education. Books can illuminate and make concepts more concrete in these vital areas of the curriculum, demonstrate relationships among the disciplines that comprise STEM, and promote integration with other subjects, such as language arts or social studies.

Figure 5.8	Teaching Idea: Science and Math Vocabulary (All Grades)

Teachers can use the books in this chapter to enhance students' vocabulary development of specialized science and math words. The class can create a "word wall" of terms associated with the various science and math topics in the books and continue to add words to it throughout the year. Students can make their own science or math dictionary of new words as they read them. Another idea is "list-group-label" in which students list the vocabulary associated with a topic, group the words that are related to each other in some way, and then label the list of words. Any given word can be grouped into more than one category.

Global books broaden students' awareness of these topics' problem-solving applications to international contexts and strengthen appreciation for other cultures' significant contributions to the fields. The next chapter focuses on the wealth of global connections with the arts, as depicted in children's books.

6

The Arts

In 1975, eight-year-old Arn was taken from his family in Cambodia by Khmer Rouge soldiers and forced to work long hours in the rice fields with little to eat. The soldiers wanted to break the painful silence of the rice fields, so Arn volunteered to learn to play the *khim*, a wooden stringed instrument struck with bamboo mallets. As he made music while the other children worked, "he thought of a world far from the pain and suffering of the work camp. Songs filled Arn's empty stomach and soothed his broken heart." Michelle Lord's (2008) account of Arn Chorn-Pond's true story in *A Song for Cambodia* illustrates the power of music to comfort and heal in tragic times. Some schools view music, dance, art, and drama as "extras" worked into the curriculum if time and resources allow. Our stance is that global children's literature about the arts is essential to understanding lives of other humans, past and present, and should be included in all areas of the curriculum as meaningful learning experiences for students.

Music and Dance

The music and dance of countries and cultures around the world are an exciting way to learn about people and places from a global perspective. Arn's story, described above, is not only a celebration of music but also a powerful description of life in the 1970s in Cambodia, when 1.7 million lives were lost during the reign of Pol Pot, leader of the Khmer Rouge. As an adult in 1998, Arn searched Cambodia for the musical masters of the past and established the Cambodian Living Arts Program to record traditional songs and teach them to a new generation. Peter Laufer's (2000) *Made in Mexico* shares the theme of celebrating local musicians. This National Geographic Society book began when Laufer's son brought back a guitar from Mexico labeled, "Paracho, Mich." Laufer flew to Mexico to investigate and found the small village of Paracho where craftsmen make guitars that rival those made in other countries in quality yet cost much less. Colorful collage illustrations by Laufer's sister, Susan Roth, have a rich textural quality made with papers, ribbons, cloth, and even shavings from crafting guitars in Paracho! The book has additional potential as a lesson in economics as readers research why the quality instruments made in Parancho sell for half the price of guitars made in other countries.

Students can learn about spicy Afro-Caribbean music and dance by reading *Salsa*, by Lillian Colón-Vilá (1998). The story is written in both English and Spanish through the voice of a young girl as she describes the musical and dancing talents of her family. There's Uncle Jorge who plays the *timbales* (Cuban drums), and Aunt Luisa who dances the salsa with elegance and a very straight back, accompanied by her husband, Pedro, on the piano. Roberta Collier-Morales' vibrant illustrations are framed by border designs befitting the text. Ballet is the focus of *Swan Lake*, retold and illustrated by Hans Christian Andersen Medal-winner Lisbeth Zwerger (2002). The author's note explains that there are actually two endings to Tchaikovsky's versions of the Andersen tale—the original "let love conquer all" ending and the tragic ending, a revision of the libretto done after Tchaikovsky's death by his brother, Modest. Zwerger explains her preference for the happy ending in this version beautifully illustrated by her oversized white-bordered paintings. The art in these two books offers opportunity for studying two different artistic styles and how the artists' decisions contributed to the meanings of each book.

Figure 6.1	Teaching Idea: Linking Music and Literature (Grades 1–5)

Before reading *Salsa*, by Lillian Colón-Vilá (1998), or *Swan Lake*, retold and illustrated by Lisbeth Zwerger (2002), ask your music teacher or local librarian to help you locate some salsa music and an audio arrangement or video of *Swan Lake*. Play the music for the class and have them write down their feelings, thoughts, and what they notice about the music and instruments. Then, when reading the books aloud to the class, have the students connect what they know about the music to the texts and illustrations. Linking the texts, art, and music will support deeper interpretations of each.

Picture-book biographies of people past and present make the lives of individual musicians and dancers accessible for readers of all ages. Jeanette Winter is the author and illustrator of several picture-book biographies discussed in this chapter—her books about artists Josefina Aguilar, Diego Rivera, Frida Kahlo, and Beatrix Potter will be a focus in the art section. Winter (1999) tells the life story of musician-composer Johann Sebastian Bach in *Sebastian: A Book About Bach*. Winter's acrylic paintings on black background perfectly illustrate how Johann heard the individual parts of instruments as he composed over 1,000 pieces before his death.

In *Two Scarlet Songbirds: A Story of Anton Dvořák*, Carole Lexa Schaefer (2001) chose to focus on a small part of the life of the famous Czech composer. Inspired by the songs of the Scarlet Tanager bird, which he heard for the first time, Dvořák composed one of his most famous pieces, *American Quartet*. Elizabeth Rosen's boldly colored paintings with thick brush strokes beautifully illustrate this fictionalized account of Dvořák's summer listening to the birds.

Tony Medina's (2009) biography of reggae composer, singer, and musician Bob Marley, *I and I: Bob Marley*, employs two-page spreads, each with a full color painting by Jesse Joshua Watson and verse on a white background. Through individual verses such as "I Am the Boy from Nine Miles" and "Music Takes Me," readers learn about the life and challenges Marley faced on his way to becoming an internationally known Jamaican musician. Notes for each verse at the end of the book further explaining events of Marley's life could support a study of ways to create poetry from a person's life. Readers could use this book as a mentor text for writing their own autobiographies in verse.

The final two picture books in this section have many similarities. Both are about dancers, one from China, the other from Cambodia, each selected to leave their homes at a young age to perfect their dancing abilities, which led to international performances. *Dancing to Freedom: The True Story of Mao's Last Dancer*, an autobiography written by Li Cunxin (2007), tells of being selected to study ballet at the Beijing Dance Academy at the age of 11, the painful separation from his family, and the hours of rehearsal. Cunxin's website (http://www.licunxin.com) features his biography, the book, and a trailer of the film of his story released in September, 2009. In *Little Sap and Monsieur Rodin*, Michelle Lord (2006) built upon the few facts known about the young Cambodian dancer, Little Sap, and her meeting with famous artist Auguste Rodin to create this fictionalized account of Little Sap's early experiences as a dancer. Themes across both books of hope over despair and the merits of hard work are worthy of discussion as well as a comparison of setting, characters, and mood.

Figure 6.2	Profile: Lulu Delacre

Delightful Latino rhymes and songs, as well as authentic Latino legends and folktales, fill Lulu Delacre's many children's books. Both an author and illustrator, Delacre was born to Argentinean parents and grew up in Puerto Rico. Delacre recalls that her interest in the arts began as a young child and that her family supported her artistic pursuits. On her homepage, at www.luludelacre.com, she shares her early memories with her Uruguayan grandmother who provided her with art materials and saved all her drawings. When her family lived in Buenos Aires, Argentina, Delacre started her formal art training in painting classes. Later, as a college student at the University of Puerto Rico, Delacre studied arts in the Fine Arts Department. She also studied photography, typography, design, and illustration at L'Ecole Supérieure d'Arts Graphiques in Paris, France. By the time she finished art school, Delacre knew that she wanted to be a children's book illustrator.

Delacre's artwork has been exhibited in many museums and galleries, such as University of Puerto Rico Art Museum, Memorial Art Gallery in New York, and Keene State College Children's Literature Gallery in New Hampshire. She also has published many children's books that reflect the rich folklore and colorful traditions of Latino culture, beginning with her first book, *Nathan and Nicholas Alexander* (1986). Delacre's work has been recognized by many children's book associations and awards. For example, *The Storyteller's Candle* (2008), written by Lucia Gonzalez, was a 2009 Pura Belpré Honor Book for both text and illustration, an ALA Notable Book, and received the Jane Addams Children's Book Honor Award. *Arrorró mi niño: Latino Lullabies and Gentle Games* (2004) was a 2006 Pura Belpré Honor Book for illustration, *Salsa Stories* (2000) made the IRA List of Outstanding International Books, *Golden Tales: Myths, Legends and Folktales From Latin America* (1996) was a Cooperative Children's Book Center Choices Book, and *The Bossy Gallito: A Traditional Cuban Folktale* (also written with Lucia Gonzalez, 1994) was a 1996 Pura Belpré Honor Book for both text and illustration.

Many of Delacre's books are available both in English and Spanish. Others, such as *Arroz con leche: Popular Songs and Rhymes from Latin America* (1989) and *Vejigante Masquerader* (1993) are Spanish-English bilingual books. Delacre notes on her homepage that she creates her bilingual books "out of love and the conviction that they are sorely needed" (Delacre, n.d., para. 1). She believes that Latino children experience a feeling of acceptance when they enjoy their language and heritage with their peers. Delacre also hopes that children see the values of keeping their culture and language through bilingual books.

The majority of Delacre's books are designed for young children, but recently she wrote a young adult novel based on the life of her daughter, Alicia. *Alicia Afterimage* (2008) is informed by interviews with Alicia's friends after she died in a car accident when she was 16. This book was the Bloomsbury Review 2008 Editor's Favorite. Currently, Delacre lives with her family in the United States and visits schools across the country. She also travels around the world to share her beloved Latino stories with children in other countries.

—*Jongsun Wee*

Music and dance reflect the cultures of the world and invite readers to learn about new customs and cultures through rhythm, movement, and melody. Many of the described books also provide excellent links to art.

Art and Artists

The Collector of Moments, by German author-illustrator Quint Buchholz (1997), links well from music to art since there are elements of both in the story line. The narrative, translated from German by Peter F. Neumeyer, focuses on the friendship between a young boy and Max, an artist who lived two flights above. The boy's violin music inspired the artist's singing and painting, but to the boy's chagrin, the paintings were always displayed with the back side out. When Max leaves, he gives the key to his place to the boy who discovers that Max had reversed all the pictures and left notes on each. Each painting, framed in white with elements of reality and fantasy, bleeds across the fold just short of Max's brief note. Finally, the boy realizes why the paintings had to be revealed when Max was gone— "The answers to all my questions were revealed in the long spells which I spent in front of the pictures." The oversized art in this book is sure to inspire interpretive discussions about the meaning viewers create as they study Max's work.

Learning to Look

Like Max, readers will need to both pose and answer their own questions when viewing images in books. Frey and Fisher (2008) define visual literacy as "the complex act of meaning making using still or moving images" (p. 1). Visual literacy creates the expectation that readers will process both text and visual elements to create meaning. Both picture books and chapter books offer such opportunities. For example, Brian Selznick's (2007) Caldecott Award-winning *The Invention of Hugo Cabret* moves between text and full-page black-and-white sketches in a movielike format over more than 500 pages to tell the story of Hugo Cabret, an orphan, clock keeper, and thief in Paris in the 1930s. Clearly, in this lengthy volume, the illustrations are key to creating meaning for the reader. (Visit http://www.theinvention ofhugocabret.com/index.htm to learn more about the creation of this book and films done by George Méliès, whose work inspired Selznick to create *Hugo Cabret*.) Black-and-white graphics are also used in

Persepolis: The Story of a Childhood as Marjane Satrapi (2003) recounts her childhood in Tehran during the overthrow of the Shah's regime. (A PG-13-rated animated film, released in 2007, combines this volume and its sequel, making it more appropriate for a mature audience.) Although some teachers focus their use of graphic novels on reluctant readers, believing that such books are more accessible for them, making meaning from these texts requires much more than reading brief speech balloons. The images require interpretation as well.

Figure 6.3	Teaching Idea: Global Artistic Techniques (Grades 1–5)

The illustrators cited in this book employ a range of techniques for students to study and try out. Those interested in watercolor could examine the works of Anno, Niki Daly, or Julie Vivas and then complete their own watercolor paintings influenced by one or more artists. Other students may want to explore the collage techniques of Ed Young or acrylic paintings done by Jeanette Winter. Studying artistic styles can be supported by the building art teacher or local artists. Students will bring new meaning to future books when they are knowledgeable about the artistic styles and techniques used by illustrators as they interpret the author's message.

Interpreting the visual aspects of global children's literature can be further complicated by cultural differences. On one hand, Garrett (2008) argues that "certain universals of expression allow children's books from one culture to be readily understood by children of another" (p. 21). However, Garrett also cites research by Masaki Yuki that Japanese readers look at the eyes to determine emotional cues, but readers in the United States focus on the mouth. Garrett concludes that "there is information encoded in illustrations that is culturally so specific that it cannot be understood outside the boundaries of a cultural group" (p. 21). Readers must avoid assuming that differences in artistic styles are not only different but perhaps less appealing than more familiar illustrations. Thus, teachers must strive to share and appreciate the illustrative styles of many cultures to teach "the child viewer that there are mysterious things out there awaiting his or her discovery" (Garrett, 2003, p. 124). When teachers and students study and respect images from global literature, they are creating meanings well beyond the text to discover subtle but important differences across countries, cultures, and lives in this global context.

Figure 6.4	Classroom Vignette: Familiar and New: Building Global Connections With What Students Know (Grades 3–5)

During a unit of study centered on China, fourth-grade teacher Tonya Salisbury and her class at Emerson World Languages and Cultures Magnet School examined China's geography and natural resources as well as its culture, history, traditions, and people. For Tonya, planning a global studies unit includes using a variety of informational and literary texts to build connections between other cultures and students' home cultures. As a part of this unit, students were led to make connections using the prose, poetry, and figurative language that describe China's geography in *Beyond the Great Mountains*, by Ed Young (2005). This book was chosen specifically because of the figurative language used in the text, the unique integration of ideographs (Chinese symbols that graphically represent abstract ideas) with the text, and the stunning illustrations that convey information about the geographic features of the country.

The lesson started as Tonya shared pictures of Chinese characters and discussed how abstract visual images and figurative language were similar. One group of students described how they accurately "read" the word horse from a character drawn with four lines and an abstract body shape, but the class found that the ideographs for *sun, mouth, seeing,* and *father* were not as easy! Tonya made the statement that "Those are not easy to visualize" and explained that in *Beyond the Great Mountains* the ideographs would be supported by illustrations and text. She further described the poetry format of the book. Poetry, she explained is not straight-forward language; they would not be reading text like, "'China has big mountains, or China has rivers.' It's not going to be simple like that. Ed Young uses the language of poetry to describe the geography of China."

After hearing the book read aloud and viewing the ideographs and the illustrations, students were asked to choose one line from the text to explain in their own words. They were directed to use resources such as a dictionary and thesaurus to help them interpret the complex meanings in the poetry and then rewrite the line in "common language."

The poem begins with the line, "Beyond the Great Mountains, Far to the East, A Vast Fertile Plain." Here is one group's clarifying translation: "In China, in the east, is a large rich flat land." Another group used the line, "As Sun, Moon Kept Watch, Earth Gave Birth, To Sprouts Above, Metal Below," and wrote, "Plants grow above ground and lots of metals form underground."

Tonya credits the past study of figurative language with supporting students' ability to think deeply and make connections between more common language and the poetic language in *Beyond the Great Mountains*. Tonya notes the success of this lesson as she describes the satisfaction all teachers can recognize, "One of the best moments you can have as a teacher is when everything you've been doing in your classroom just seems to fit together and your students can see the connections."

Teacher: Tonya Salisbury, Grade 4, Westerville, Ohio

Writer: Marlene Beierle, Dublin, Ohio

Looking Closely

One way to explore visual elements from a global perspective is to study books that focus on international artists, past and present. French author, Caroline Desnoëttes (2006), created a "lift-and-learn" book, *Look Closer: Art Masterpieces Through the Ages*. Famous paintings of the past are featured on the left page, with sections enlarged on the right to give readers that closer look. By lifting the flap in the center, readers are directed to look specifically at parts of the painting and learn more about the painting's background. Lifting the flap on the right reveals the artist's palette through circles taken directly from the painting. The book's format encourages both interaction and conversation.

London author, Lucy Micklethwait (1995), has designed a collection of books for children of all ages to encourage them to look closely at highly regarded pieces of art. For the youngest readers, for example, Micklethwait's *Spot a Cat: A Child's Book of Art* is a collection of art from the 1400s to the 1950s, which have a cat as part of each composition. On the left, readers find a question that encourages them to find the cat in the art on the right. Similarly, in *Colors: A First Art Book*, Micklethwait (2005) organized art around the topic of color with two pieces of art for each color and simple labels such as "blue sky" and "blue sea." For older art enthusiasts, Micklethwait's (1992) *I Spy: An Alphabet in Art* asks readers to play the "I spy" game on each two-page spread to find an object with a different letter of the alphabet. Micklethwait's *I Spy a Freight Train: Transportation in Art* (1996) plays the same game with trains, cars, and other methods of transportation. Each book invites readers to see pieces of art more closely and will encourage conversation as readers share their discoveries.

How can a blind person "look closely" at art? It is fitting to close this section with an exceptional book first published in Mexico before being translated into English. *The Black Book of Colors*, by Menena Cottin (2006), won the New Horizons prize at the Bologna Children's Book Fair in 2007, and its title inspires considerable anticipation of the book's contents. How can there be a black book of colors? In fact, every page is black. Yes, the text is written in white, but it is also in Braille, which helps readers touch, smell, and even taste colors. For example, "Brown crunches under his feet like fall leaves. Sometimes it smells like chocolate, and other times it stinks" is on the left page, and raised illustrations on the right on shiny black paper enable the reader to also feel the art and make the color meaningful. This translated book offers new insights into how to "see" color and art from a diverse perspective.

| **Figure 6.5** | Teaching Idea: "Seeing" Colors With Words (Grades 1–3) |

Before reading *The Black Book of Colors* (Cottin, 2006), challenge the class to describe a color without using other color words. Try to write a description of one color as a group, paying particular attention to the words that are most descriptive. Then, have the students work in pairs or individually to select a color and create a description. During sharing time, see if the rest of the class can guess the color. This writing experience will not only support the writers' skills using descriptive language but will also support their appreciation of the author's craft when you read *The Black Book of Colors*.

Art and Poetry

Art inspired poetry in the next three books. In *Paint Me a Poem*, Justine Rowden (2005) selected an international collection of art from the National Gallery of Art in Washington, D.C., and created a wide assortment of poems for each. The curls of the woman in da Vinci's *Ginevra de' Benci* are celebrated with a concrete poem with the words literally "whirling/swirling/chasing/racing." Additional notes about each artist are provided as well as a challenge to teachers and students to write poetry based on their interpretations of art. Visit http://www.paintmeapoem.com to listen to music selected for several of the pages, then select just the right songs for other poems in the book! Jan Greenberg's (2008) *Side by Side: New Poems Inspired by Art From Around the World* is a collection of varied art (sculpture, paintings, photography, ceramic figures, and even a coffin!), each of which inspired a poem that is presented in both the poet's language and an English translation. The art–poem pairings are thoughtfully organized according to stories, voices, expressions, and impressions followed by biographies of the poets, translators, and artists. Famous artists who illustrate children's literature around the world contributed to *Under the Spell of the Moon*, a collection of art, rhymes, songs, riddles, street games, and poetry edited by Patricia Aldana (2004), with proceeds benefiting the International Board on Books for Young People (IBBY). Many of the poems are available in both their original language and English.

| **Figure 6.6** | Teaching Idea: Poems Inspired by Art (All Grades) |

Share poems from either *Paint Me a Poem* by Justine Rowden (2005) or Jan Greenberg's (2008) *Side by Side: New Poems Inspired by Art from Around the World*, and discuss the connections between the poem and the artwork. Then, select several pieces of art, either contemporary or classic, to inspire students to write their own poems. Pictures of artwork, selected by students from the Internet, could be added to their final poems to illustrate their work. These finished projects can be displayed in a classroom Art and Poetry Gallery.

In *The House*, with art by Italian Roberto Innocenti and poems by J. Patrick Lewis (2009), the simple, two-word title and Innocenti's powerful cover art invite the reader to wonder about "the house" . . . What is this book about? Who are these people? How are they related to the house? A single page of text in the voice of the house in the present day (but built in 1656) foreshadows that the reader will learn much about the history of the house. Readers are immersed in the art, answering some questions and creating new ones as they study the house and the people in the illustrations over time. Poetry has a universal quality and could be illustrated in many ways, but the marriage of Lewis's quatrains with Innocenti's art creates a true picture book as the combination offers a meaning greater than either alone.

These collections of two art forms—illustration and poetry—are not only visions of people, places, and cultures from around the world but are also important models for readers' own artistic creations in either word or media.

Biographies of Artists

Both picture books and chapter books are available to support a study of individual artists, such as Vincent van Gogh, for example. Susan Goldman Rubin's (2001) *The Yellow House* focuses on a single summer of van Gogh's life that he spent with Paul Gauguin in a yellow house in Arles in the south of France. This book will inspire readers to investigate more about both painters, perhaps through the chapter book by Jan Greenberg and Sandra Jordan (2001), *Vincent van Gogh: Portrait of an Artist*. Words, rather than color, paint this portrait beginning with van Gogh's birth in 1853. Each chapter describes several years in van Gogh's life, including one that offers greater detail about the summer with Paul Gauguin. With the background of both books, readers would be well positioned to read Neil Waldman's (1999) *The Starry Night*, a fictionalized account of what might have happened if a young boy met van Gogh in Central Park and took the artist on a tour of New York City. Waldman's art is clearly inspired by van Gogh's famous painting *The Starry Night*.

Fans of Marc Chagall might start with Michelle Markel's (2005) *Dreamer From the Village*, which begins with Chagall's birth in a Russian village and ends with a show of his paintings in the Louvre at the age of 90. Emily Lisker's illustrations lean on Chagall's paintings in both color and form, which could inspire readers to create their own art pieces informed by the masterpieces they study.

Originally published in French, Marie Sellier's (1996) *Chagall from A to Z* provides an alphabetic look at Chagall's life. F, for example, is for his fiancée, Bella, who misses Marc during their four years of separation before marrying. Each letter offers a two-page spread of both text and Chagall's paintings. Deeper insights into Chagall's childhood are explored in a brief chapter book by Eric A. Kimmel (2007), *A Picture for Marc*. Readers learn that Chagall's desire to become an artist at first was discouraged by his father. The range of books available about artists such as van Gogh and Chagall ensure that children of all ages and reading ability can discover famous artists and share the perspectives of these unique books with the rest of the class. Eric Kimmel's website (http://www.ericakimmel.com) features a blog and teacher guides to many of his books with discussion questions and learning activities.

Students studying Mexico and its artists will want to read books by Jonah Winter and his mother, Jeanette Winter. *Josefina*, written by Jeanette Winter (1996), celebrates the life of Josefina Aguilar and her love of clay in the form of a counting book. The mother-son team collaborated on *Diego* (written by Jonah Winter, 1991), a bilingual book on the childhood and artistry of Diego Rivera. Jonah Winter's (2002) picture-book biography of Rivera's wife, Frida Kahlo, is simply titled *Frida*, illustrated by Ana Juan, a native of Spain. The book describes the tragic accident that left Kahlo in constant pain; yet, her painting continued as she became a celebrated Mexican artist and an inspiration to women artists all over the world.

Becoming an Artist

How-to books can help readers who want to try the techniques of famous artists. Joyce Raimondo's (2005) *Express Yourself!: Activities and Adventures in Expressionism* explains the specific characteristics of painters like Dutch artist van Gogh or German painter Ernst Ludwig Kirchner in ways that encourage children to try it themselves! Similarly, *Art Around the World: Loo-Loo, Boo, and More Art You Can Do*, by Denis Roche (1998), takes readers on a global adventure learning about artistic media, like weaving from Mexico, mosaics from Italy, and block prints from India. Readers interested in the ancient arts of Japan can learn about sword making, basket weaving, puppet designs, and more in Sheila Hamanaka and Ayano Ohmi's (1999) *In Search of the Spirit: The Living National Treasures of Japan*. Each chapter is based upon a Japanese artist, identified as a "Living National

Treasure," and includes photographs and a description of the artists and their crafts. Aspiring artists will enjoy learning about the young life of Wang Yani, a Chinese artist who began painting at the age of three in *A Young Painter*, by Zheng Zhensun and Alice Low (1991). This informational book offers examples of Yani's art on every page and follows her work from ages 3 to 16.

Stories About Art and Artists

Fictional stories are also a genre to explore to learn about art and artists around the world. Karen Lynn Williams (1998) takes readers to Haiti and introduces them to Ti Marie, a young aspiring painter in *Painted Dreams*, and her determination against the odds. Ti Marie wants desperately to paint, but her family has no money for paints until Ti Marie scrapes off the moss on the wall behind the stall where Mama sells her vegetables and creates a picture that draws admirers to look at the picture and buy Mama's produce. Readers will learn about the Chinese New Year and stone carving in *A Gift*, by Yong Chen (2009). Amy is excited to discover that her uncles, far away in China, have sent her a gift to celebrate the Chinese New Year. Illustrations by the author help young readers to follow the changes in setting and the flashback story of the necklace. Both books encourage readers to see art all around them. Ti Marie created art from a blank wall, and Amy's uncle did the same from a simple stone.

Matteo Pericoli (2008) sets *Tommaso and the Missing Line* in his home country, Italy. Young artist, Tommaso, is missing a line from his drawing of a house on a hill near his grandma. He looks everywhere for it and begins to see many lines—a dog's leash, the curl of a cat's tail, and a car's antenna. Pericoli effectively focuses readers' attention on line through black-and-white line drawings accented with a single line of orange on appropriate pages. Finally, readers travel to South Africa in Niki Daly's (2009) first chapter book, *Bettina Valentino and the Picasso Club*, in which the new art teacher, Mr. Popart, teaches readers along with his students about famous artists.

Drama

Many of the books in this volume can stimulate drama activities in the classroom. For example, Ole Könnecke's (2006) *Anthony and the Girls*, described in Chapter 3, could be dramatized with Anthony trying all sorts of antics to get the attention of the girls in the sandbox.

Some attempts could be close to those in the book, but others could be imagined! Since the book ends as a new friend approaches, children could also dramatize what might happen next. *The Color of My Words* by Lynn Joseph (2000), also in Chapter 3, could be the backdrop for role-playing in the form of a debate central to the plot. One side might argue for new buildings on the land as a sign of progress while the other side could be environmentalists who want the oceanfront land to remain pristine. Nathalie Dieterlé's (2001) *I am the King!*, translated from French, features a young rabbit pretending to be a king and taking it a little too far—the king will not go to school, take a bath, or eat anything but chocolate. His parents convince him to stop being a king, so instead, he becomes a wolf! Children will enjoy dramatizing each of the rabbit's characters and creating new ones as they imagine what the little rabbit may pretend to be next.

Plays are excellent ways for children to dramatize the meaning of a text. For example, Lori Marie Carlson (1999) selected seven plays written by playwrights from Spain, Latin America, and the United States for her book, *You're On! Seven Plays in English and Spanish*. These short pieces not only provide for valuable reading and listening experiences but also offer performative opportunities as well. Students can assume individual parts and prepare to interpret their character using appropriate tone, inflection, and cadence while reading their part aloud as a reader's theater to the rest of the class. Because each play is available in English and Spanish, there are many opportunities to learn about each language. These plays also can instigate learning more about the playwrights' countries.

A variety of books have been written about one of the most famous British playwrights—William Shakespeare. Three versions of his life in picture-book format provide opportunities for comparison in terms of content and style. *Bard of Avon: The Story of William Shakespeare*, written by Diane Stanley and Peter Vennema (1992), begins in Shakespeare's childhood, a time when his family lived in fear of his father's arrest for not paying his taxes. The text moves rapidly to Shakespeare's life as an adult, when the theatre was central to English life at that time. Readers also learn about the workings of the theatre as depicted in full-page paintings by Stanley. British author Michael Rosen's (2001) biography, *Shakespeare: His Work & His World*, is an oversized chapter book with single- and double-page illustrations by Australian Robert Ingpen. Each chapter focuses on a slice of Shakespeare's life and includes quotes from various Shakespearian plays. Finally, Aliki's (1999) *William Shakespeare & the Globe* presents Shakespeare's life as a series of acts and scenes, illustrated with colored pencil drawings.

Gary Blackwood (1998, 2000, 2003) has written a series of three award-winning fictional chapter books about a poor orphan boy, Widge, who works his way into the Globe Theatre and also into the life of William Shakespeare. In the first, *The Shakespeare Stealer*, Widge's talents at shorthand are employed by his ruthless master to write the scripts of plays in secret so they can be performed with higher profit outside of London. The Black Plague strikes London in the sequel, *Shakespeare's Scribe*, so Widge has joined the troupe and left London to perform plays across England. When Shakespeare injures his arm, Widge uses his shorthand skills to write plays as Shakespeare dictates. In the final volume, *Shakespeare's Spy*, a thief is stealing from the troupe. When Widge is suspected, he becomes a spy to solve the mystery and clear his name.

Figure 6.7	Teaching Idea: Character Development Across Texts and Time (Grades 4–6+)

Gary Blackwood's (1998, 2000, 2003) novels set in Shakespeare's time are opportunities to study character development across texts and time as several main characters appear in all of the books. One group of students may want to study Shakespeare himself to identify how readers learn more about the Bard with each successive novel. Another group could use reference materials to identify which of Shakespeare's character traits are factual and which are probably fictional. The young boy, Widge, may be studied by yet another group to see how Blackwood develops this fictional character over time. Each group could share their findings using drama—an interview with Widge, a scene with Shakespeare as the main character, or a portrayal of an author of a book about Shakespeare explaining the sources used for writing the Bard's biography.

Another fictional account about Shakespeare is *The Boy, the Bear, the Baron, the Bard*, by Australian Gregory Rogers (2004). This wordless book asks the question, What if a young boy time-traveled to Shakespeare's theater, was chased out of the Globe by Shakespeare, rescued a bear from a cage, and helped a baron about to be executed escape? This oversized picture book will delight young readers with the character's antics through pen-and-ink illustrations colored with watercolors. Some books present Shakespeare's plays in unique formats to make them more accessible for children. Marcia Williams (1998, 2000), for example, created *Tales from Shakespeare* and *More Tales from Shakespeare*, using an oversized comic book format with seven plays in each book. The action in each frame is summarized in the text below it with the actors' lines written above their heads.

Conclusion

We close this chapter with a biography of Danish author, actor, and singer Hans Christian Andersen. Hjørdis Varmer (2005) is a popular children's author in Denmark known for thoroughly researching her topics. Her biography of Andersen, *Hans Christian Andersen: His Fairy Tale Life,* was endorsed by the Danish committee in charge of celebrating Andersen's life at the Han Christian Andersen Bicentennial 2005. Chapters are colorfully illustrated by Danish illustrator Lilian Brøgger, who included many of Andersen's own drawings in her art. Andersen's spirit for the arts is consistent with the intent of this chapter, encouraging teachers to celebrate the lives of artists, musicians, writers, dancers, and actors—both famous and those in their own classrooms. This chapter also concludes Part 1, which has focused on ways to infuse global literature throughout the curriculum. In the final section, we turn to issues that teachers may face as you seek to incorporate more global literature in your classroom instruction.

"*Inspiring and moving.*" — NELSON MANDELA

The Day Gogo Went to Vote

by Elinor Batezat Sisulu
Illustrated by Sharon Wilson

One of the many wonderful children's books described in *Reading Globally, K–8*.

PART II

Issues Teachers Face

Katherine Paterson, Newbery medalist and Hans Christian Andersen Award recipient, has added the Library of Congress honor of National Ambassador for Young People's Literature for 2010 to 2011 to her long list of recognitions. Her 2009 novel, *The Day of the Pelican*, was inspired by experiences of a refugee family from Kosovo who immigrated to Paterson's hometown in Vermont. A longtime friend of international literature organizations such as the International Board on Books for Young People, Paterson spoke at the eighth IBBY Regional Conference session, "Hans Christian Andersen Authors Speak Out," on October 3, 2009, and issued a call to action for the conference attendees. On likening the conference to a "social contagion," Paterson said,

> This weekend I'm catching all kinds of good things from friends near and far, and when we go home tomorrow, we'll be spreading this contagion and enthusiasm for bringing books to children all over the globe. None of us would be here today except for children's books . . . . One way [our children] can have friends in other countries . . . is by giving them books that bring other lands and cultures alive . . . . It's contagious. Go spread the contagion!

Attending conferences such as this is important professional development for all of us who work with children and literacy. However, what happens sometimes when teachers (such as you, our readers) learn new ideas at a professional conference, inservice, graduate course, or from reading a text like this one? If your experiences are anything like ours were, you return to your classroom energized and enthusiastic. Then suddenly reality hits, and you are confronted with many questions. We have anticipated (based upon our experience) what some of those questions might be. In the first place, global books are not always easily accessible. We have tried to include titles that we know can be purchased in the United States online and may be available in libraries, but still it can be challenging to locate some. Once you do find a particular title or perhaps others we don't mention, how should you evaluate them if they are unfamiliar to you? How will you obtain the funds to purchase new books? What if controversies arise around a certain title? How can you justify using this literature to meet curricular standards? We raise—and try to answer—these and other similar questions in this section. If you are reading this book in a professional development setting or on your own, generate a list of your own questions and concerns at this point. Then, read our final section, discuss with colleagues the solutions we offer, identify any questions left unanswered, and brainstorm your own solutions or how you would modify the ones we propose. Make this an interactive professional learning experience between our ideas and you and your colleagues!

7

How Should I Evaluate Global Books?

British author Elizabeth Laird (1991, 2004, 2006) typically writes about cultures other than her own: the Kurds of Iraq in *Kiss the Dust*, an Ethiopian friendship between two boys in *The Garbage King*, and Palestinians under Israeli occupation in *A Little Piece of Ground*, among others. She has traveled widely and lived in such diverse locations as Ethiopia, Malaysia, India, Iraq, and Lebanon. She has won awards for her books. Yet, if I am an American teacher and perhaps unfamiliar with many of these countries, how should I judge these books? On which global titles should I spend my precious book budget? Which books should I select to use in my classroom?

In this chapter, we consider these kinds of questions. In particular, we address two broad areas in book selection: authenticity of global books and literary quality. Specific issues we discuss include the author's background, qualifications, and point of view; the importance of accuracy; how to recognize stereotyping through characters, language, and illustrations; the perspective of readers from within the culture; literary merit; and issues of translation. We also present a rubric organizing all these criteria into one format that we hope teachers will find useful in guiding their selections.

How can I know if these books are authentic?

Perhaps the most fundamental consideration in evaluation and selection of global books is authenticity. No matter how good otherwise, if a
book fails in this respect, we need to rethink if or how it may be used
with students (Cai, 2002). Writing about multicultural, as opposed to
global, literature, critic Mingshui Cai states, "What I term cultural cor-
rectness must be the basic criterion for evaluating multicultural literature, if we are to maintain the cultural integrity of the people
represented in it" (p. 87). This issue is especially critical given our fairly
inclusive definition of global literature in this book. We incorporate not
only literature first published in other countries and literature written
by authors from other countries and first published in the United States
but also literature written by immigrants to the United States about their
home countries and by U. S. authors with settings in other countries. In
this text, we have tried to include books that are culturally authentic, but
we urge readers to consider all books carefully in the following ways.

First, what is the author's background? Authenticity begins with
the author, which includes status as an insider or outsider of the culture being represented in the book, because being an insider certainly
gives the writer more credibility for understanding cultural subtleties,
not just obvious surface features. However, insider-outsider status is
relative; that is, someone who has lived entirely within the culture is
more an insider than someone who has lived in the culture for an
extended time, who in turn is more an insider than someone who has
visited the culture for a short period, who then is more an insider than
someone who relies only on research to learn about a culture. For
example, Bolormaa Baasansuren (2009), author of *My Little Round
House*, was born and currently resides in Mongolia, while Tololwa M.
Mollel (1999), author of *My Rows and Piles of Coins*, born in Tanzania
and living there until adulthood, now resides in Canada. Jane Kurtz
(1997), author of several books set in Ethiopia, such as *Trouble*, grew up
in that country after her family moved there when she was two years
old but now lives in the United States. Karen Lynn Williams, writer of
stories set in Haiti (see subsequent discussion), lived there for two
years. Finally, Ted Lewin examplifies an author who has traveled
widely and written books, such as *Horse Song: The Naadam of Mongolia*
(co-authored with Betsy Lewin, 2008), that are inspired by the places
he has visited and researched. (Compare this book with Baasansuren's
My Little Round House.) Although being an insider does not automati-
cally ensure that a book will be authentic, not to mention well-written,
"when the author's ethnicity differs from that portrayed in the book,

there may be special, albeit unintentional, problems with accuracy that would be conveyed to readers" (Lehman, 2006, p. 14).

Thus, part of judging the authenticity of culturally similar books, such as Canadian author Deborah Ellis's (2000, 2002, 2003) trilogy set in Afghanistan and Pakistan—*The Breadwinner, Parvana's Journey*, and *Mud City*—and Pakistani-Canadian author Rukhsana Khan's (2009) *Wanting Mor*, set in Afghanistan, is assessing the insider status of the authors. Ellis's inspiration for the *Breadwinner* trilogy came from time she spent in Afghan refugee camps in Pakistan, and she donates royalties from this set to two charitable organizations that work with Afghan women and street children. Khan, born in Pakistan, has lived in Canada since the age of three. She credits her Afghan sister-in-law with providing cultural insights and two other individuals from Afghanistan with checking the manuscript for accuracy. Her fluency with Muslim practices and religious language reflects her own deep immersion in that community. Learning about the authors helps us begin to gauge the potential authenticity of their books.

Figure 7.1	Profile: Rukhsana Khan

Rukhsana Khan is both an author and storyteller best known for the openness with which she shares her Muslim culture. Born in Lahore, Pakistan, her family immigrated to Dundas, Canada, in the mid-1960s when she was three. Her father, a tool-and-die maker, wanted to move someplace where his daughter would be given the same opportunities as male children. At that time, the small town was very homogeneous, and prejudice toward outsiders was very strong. Her family suffered cruel teasing both in her father's work place and at her school from people who could not accept their different appearance and traditions.

Most of Khan's inspiration for writing seems to stem from these childhood experiences. Not only did the hostilities of her classmates drive her to escape into story, but also their lack of understanding pushed her to write about her faith for readers across Canada and the United States. Of her books, *Muslim Child: Understanding Islam through Stories and Poems* (1999) is the most straightforward presentation of Islam, quoting the Quran—Islam's central religious text—and using poems, parables, and explanatory sidebars to discuss dress, dietary restrictions, celebrations, and history, in addition to the five pillars of Islam.

As an insider to the Muslim faith, Khan feels she can convey a more authentic experience than someone who applies an outsider's sensibilities, usually white or feminist, upon the subject. Indeed, *Wanting Mor* (2009), a novel about a partially disfigured Muslim girl in Afghanistan, depicts realistic conditions, carefully presenting both positive and negative sides. For example, American soldiers are portrayed as both destructive and benevolent. Mirroring Khan's beliefs, religion serves as a lens through which the world is constantly evaluated, imparting both comfort and challenges that strengthen the believer.

(Continued)

(Continued)

Khan's picture books range from stories that present universal experiences such as sibling rivalry, trying to fall asleep, and courage, to those that directly address the experience of children in the Middle East. Both *Ruler of the Courtyard* (2003) and *Silly Chicken* (2005) maintain their links to Khan's cultural viewpoint through their setting in Pakistan. On the other hand, *The Roses in My Carpets* (1998) and *King of the Skies* (2001) present the conditions of Afghan refugee camps, the effects of conflict upon children, and dealing with a disability.

Now living in multicultural Toronto with her husband, daughters, and son, Khan's greatest strength is her willingness to candidly discuss the religion that has formed the core of her life. When the author has encountered reoccurring issues such as the prohibition of physical contact with members of the opposite sex or ignorance about the needs of Muslim visitors she has responded by writing clear and gentle articles about these topics on her website (www.rukhsanakhan.com). In the classroom, her writings offer teachers valuable resources with which to help build bridges between Muslims and readers, especially as real-life interactions between the followers of Islam and non-Muslims increase with western interactions in the Middle Eastern world.

—Erin Reilly-Sanders

However, an author's background also includes other experiences and qualifications, such as education, travel, expertise on the book's topic, and literary recognition. For example, Christine Taylor-Butler (2009), the author of *Sacred Mountain Everest*, mentioned in Chapter 5, graduated from Massachusetts Institute of Technology, an educational background that may qualify her to write a science-related book such as this. Yet the book jacket, online reviews of the book, and her own website do not reveal whether she ever visited Mount Everest to witness the things about which she writes. On the other hand, Katie Smith Milway (2008), author of *One Hen*—also cited in Chapter 5, "coordinated community development programs in Africa . . . for Food for the Hungry International," according to the book jacket. In addition, the Kids Can Press website (www.kidscanpress .com/Canada/CreatorDetails.aspx?cid=200) states, "She was a delegate to the 1992 Earth Summit and has authored two books and numerous articles on sustainable development and served as a resource specialist to the Salzburg Global Seminar" (Kids Can Press, n.d., para. 2). Finally, we also see on the website the literary awards this book has received, including selection for the USBBY Outstanding International Books and the IRA Notable Books for a Global Society lists in 2009. These details lend credibility to the author's knowledge and qualifications regarding the book and her literary recognition.

An author's writing style always conveys a point of view or attitude about the topic—in this case, the culture—being portrayed in the book. That perspective, most clearly revealed by the book's tone, can reflect the author's insider-outsider status and the author's vision of the book's intended audience. For example, two books cited earlier— *The Breadwinner* (Ellis, 2000) and *Wanting Mor* (Khan, 2009)—make a good comparison of this point. From her experiences with Afghan refugees, Deborah Ellis conveys a sympathetic attitude for their plight under the Taliban regime, which she describes in an author's note as "extremely restrictive" towards women and girls. The solution to Parvana's situation is to escape—as depicted in subsequent books in the trilogy. That attitude (sympathetic and shocked) probably matches her intended audience well, as North Americans typically have a very different view of the status of females. Rukhsana Khan (author of *Wanting Mor*) also is an outsider regarding Afghanistan. However, she does have close ties with cultural insiders, and as a Muslim herself conveys a different attitude toward Afghan women's and girls' status. Granted that her story is set after the fall of the Taliban, but the treatment of females, while still repressive by Western standards, receives a more contextualized and nuanced cast from within a Muslim perspective. Indeed, Khan seems to envision her audience as, if not Muslim, at least willing to be educated about their practices. Thus, readers should consider an author's attitude or perspective as part of evaluating a book's authenticity.

Related to authenticity, accuracy is critical in evaluating global books. In a very insightful text, *Representing Africa in Children's Literature*, scholar Vivian Yenika-Agbaw (2008) critiques numerous children's and young adult books about that continent. One example that she cites, Ann Grifalconi's (2002) *The Village That Vanished*, portrays a Yao village's response to the news that slavers are coming. However, as Yenika-Agbaw notes, the story does not identify the specific slave trade being depicted in the story, and the fact that the slavers shown in the illustrations are black can imply that they were the only ones involved in the slave trade. This is an example of *omission:* Beyond inaccuracies that are *included*, important *omitted* information causes additional concern. We observe that also the book never states the location of the Yao village (in present-day Malawi and Tanzania) and that the author's note provides little information and refers to Africa in a generic sense, not as a continent made up of many countries. Thus, accuracy both in what *is* presented and what *isn't* requires careful scrutiny and often extra research on the reader's part. When an author adds information and lists resources, including books and consultants, readers can feel more confident about its trustworthiness, but without such aids, the task of evaluation is much harder.

One particular aspect of accuracy—stereotyping—can be enormously challenging for readers outside a culture to recognize. For example, Yenika-Agbaw (2008) also criticizes Grifalconi's (2002) book cited above and her work more generally for its stereotypical portrayal of the villagers' reliance on ancestral worship and supernatural events to deliver them from danger. The setting in this book and others by the same author also reinforces exotic stereotypes that many Westerners have of African life as rural, and the lack of a specific location also conforms to our undifferentiated view of Africa as monolithic.

How characters are portrayed through story and illustration also can contribute to stereotypes. For example, in Diane Wolkstein's *Bouki Dances the Kokioko* (1997), this well-known reteller of folktales from around the world introduces American readers to two famous Haitian characters: fat and gullible or stupid Bouki and cunning, malicious Malice. These character types may reinforce outsiders' views of black persons, but the illustrations are even more troubling, as critiqued in some reviews. Created by Jesse Sweetwater, they depict these characters as very dark, with wide white eyes and large red lips. Although one double-page spread does portray a group of characters ranging in hue from golden to dark, they all exhibit exaggerated, rather comical physical features. We have to question what image of Haitians we gain from viewing these images. Do they represent the full range of physical features expected in that cultural environment? Thus, when evaluating books for authenticity, it is important to carefully examine their representation of characters.

Another problematic aspect of stereotyping is the relationships between characters, particularly those from different cultures. Which characters have more power? When power relationships conform to stereotypes of racial, ethnic, and class dominance, we should be especially wary. For example, in *Mud City*, the Deborah Ellis (2003) book cited earlier, Shauzia is rescued from the streets of Peshawar, Pakistan, by a Western family who takes her to live with them for a short while until they reach the limit of their patience with her "foreign" ways. This relationship may reinforce two kinds of stereotypes: The first is that globally poor people need to be rescued by well-off Westerners; and second, those same rescuers may tire of doing so and abandon the needy. Luckily for Shauzia, a fellow Afghan, Mrs. Weera, a female authority figure who runs the refugee camp compound, ultimately shows Shauzia how to control her own destiny.

For outsiders to the cultures portrayed in most global books, getting the perspectives of readers from within the culture or with more expertise on the country being depicted often provides the most help in determining authenticity. How do they perceive the book? Do they view it as an accurate depiction, or do they recognize problems that readers outside the culture might overlook? For example, in evaluating the art of *Bouki Dances the Kokioko* (Wolkstein, 1997), we can read on the jacket flap that Sweetwater researched Haitian history, culture, and art, and other reviews have lauded the illustrations' reflection of Haitian primitivist art. While we certainly assume that the illustrator's intention was to honor Haitian culture, the best evaluation would come from Haitians themselves, as described in Figure 7.2 by our colleague Cheryl Canada, who works with teachers in Haiti. Her experience with the use of that book and with *Painted Dreams*, by Karen Lynn Williams (1998), is most enlightening.

Figure 7.2	Classroom Vignette: A Personal Lesson in Evaluating Global Literature (Classroom Teachers)

I do teacher development work in Haiti, and during one of my reading workshops with Haitian teachers, I read aloud two books to demonstrate how to read aloud to children and the ways literature can be used to gain diverse responses from children. I was careful to select books I thought were culturally relevant, choosing two books written by U.S. authors who have lived in and written about Haiti based on their experiences. I felt confident that *Painted Dreams*, by Karen Lynn Williams (1998), was an excellent choice because it reflected some of my first-hand experiences in Haiti. I also used *Bouki Dances the Kokioko*, by Diane Wolkstein (1997), because I knew Wolkstein had lived among Haitians for a few years collecting oral stories from the people in villages. Thus, I believed both books were culturally relevant and would be appreciated by the Haitian teachers.

After reading *Painted Dreams*, I asked the teachers for personal responses to the book. Some of the responses given by the teachers were:

This was a very good story.

Ti Marie's character was believable because she performed typical chores of Haitian children.

Mama was believable too because in rural Haiti life is hard, and there isn't money for things like paint supplies.

The story contained the message that you should never give up on your dream. You should believe in yourself and always persevere.

The Haitian teachers' responses confirmed my notion that *Painted Dreams* is a culturally relevant piece of literature that authentically represents life in rural Haiti.

As I read *Bouki Dances the Kokioko*, I noticed that the teachers seemed to be enjoying the story, laughing and whispering to one another as I read. Again I asked for personal responses, and I was astounded by what I heard.

(Continued)

(Continued)

> Yes, this can be a Haitian story because Bouki stories are told all over Haiti throughout our history. We all laughed at the story because it is funny on the surface, but Bouki stories have a hidden meaning that goes back to slavery here in Haiti. Bouki represents the black, stupid slave and Malice represents the white, smart slave owner who always takes advantage of the stupid slave.
>
> The faces of all the teachers immediately became somber as Marar spoke. Then Donay piped in,
> Another thing, the illustrator paints a very negative picture of Haitian people with his exaggerated characters. They all have very black skin, huge eyes, big lips and big butts. This is not the way Haitians really look. These pictures represent a stereotype about Haitians and other black people, and it's offensive!
>
> This experience taught me how important it is to gain the perspective of readers from a particular culture when evaluating the authenticity of a piece of global literature.
>
> Teacher: Cheryl L. Canada, Teacher Educator, Mansfield, Ohio

Another way to gain a reader's perspective is to imagine how we would feel regarding a book written about our own country, culture, ethnicity, or socioeconomic class. Would we be offended if similar depictions of characters, relationships, settings, attitudes, practices, beliefs, and language seem stereotyped or condescending? We need to always try to see *the other side,* as exemplified in Jacqueline Woodson's (2001) book by the same title. In this picture book, told from a black girl's point of view, we witness how she gradually befriends a white girl living on the other side of a fence that neither one of them is allowed to cross. They defy the rule by sitting together *on* the fence, as they weren't ordered not to do that. From the fence, they "can see all over" and watch "the whole wide world," symbolic of how global books will expand our vision—if we open ourselves to the possibilities.

What else do I need to know to make good book selections?

Teachers also need to examine literary merit in making good selections, because a poorly written book has questionable value, as well. In evaluating literary merit, teachers may rely upon recommendations from librarians, published reviews of books in professional publications or online, or award winners. These are excellent, time-saving sources of information (although sometimes hard to locate for international titles), but you also can judge literary merit for yourself as you read books. In the United States, generally accepted standards for evaluating fiction include an interesting, original, credible, well-constructed *plot*; an identifiable *setting* that contributes to the story's authenticity; worthwhile *themes* that avoid didacticism and arise naturally; believable, consistent, well-developed *characters*; an engaging *style* that complements the tone and other story elements; and an appropriate *point of view* from which the story is told (Kiefer, 2010). If the book is illustrated, the quality of the artwork, its appropriateness for the content, its contribution to the story, and the overall design of the book are additional considerations. Furthermore, criteria differ for nonfiction books, namely, accuracy of the information, adequacy of content, objectivity and identification of the author's perspective, organization, clarity, and format (Kiefer, 2010). Keeping these criteria in mind as we read helps us to think more critically and analytically about books beyond whether we personally *like* them or not.

However, we also must recognize that these criteria are culturally embedded, reflecting a white, Western, largely male-dominated literary tradition. Other cultures have different literary values and cultural norms. For example, various countries view the purposes of literature and reading differently—some take an aesthetic stance, while others see literature primarily as an educational, even didactic tool. In the latter, for example, moralizing (against which we've cautioned) is seen as a positive value. Furthermore, different literary traditions have various ways of "storying." That is, narrative structures may differ from what we expect and might even seem unappealing to our tastes in literature. As an example, Freeman and Lehman (2001) cite Josef Holub's *The Robber and Me* (1997), a book originally published in Germany. They note that in this book, "the plot may appear to meander at considerable length through seemingly disconnected scenes that are hard to distinguish as real or fantasy before finally beginning to reveal itself in a more straightforward manner well past the halfway point" (p. 28). Thus, we may negatively evaluate a book based upon our *cultural* literary biases, rather than so-called objective *universal* standards. There's little we can do about this, except to recognize the possibility of cultural bias and try to educate our tastes as broadly as possible by reading widely—globally—and outside our own literary tradition.

Applying Criteria While Reading

How can I apply literary criteria to evaluate a book's merit? We offer an example of a critical reading here to demonstrate how this might be done. Suppose I am a fifth- or sixth-grade teacher searching for literature to bring a global perspective to my social studies curriculum. I discover South African author Lesley Beake's (1995) *Song of Be*, a novel about a Namibian Bushmen girl caught between her traditional culture and the modern world, which sounds like it might hold promise for connections with topics we are studying. I read the book to examine its appropriateness for my class and curricular objective.

An author's note introduces the *setting* and helps me get my bearings geographically, historically, and culturally. Beake further develops the setting through Be's memories of her life in the village where she lived with her mother. However, I will need to research further to better understand the Bushmen—Be is of the Ju/'hoan people—and their culture (more on this later). By the third page of the novel, I am searching for a good map online of Namibia to find the location of Gobabis, the district of the story's setting. I find Gobabis approximately 150 miles east of Windhoek, the capital city. From the author's note, I also learn that the setting's time period occurs as the country is gaining its independence from South Africa, which, I also discover from searching online, places it between about 1988 and 1990.

The first thing I notice about the book's narrative *style* is the introductory sentence: "I have just killed myself" (p. 3), which immediately grabs my attention. How can this happen, I wonder? How can a story begin with the first person narrator's suicide? Furthermore, with such a start, will I enjoy this story? Then, I notice the use of italics to signify the present and standard print for flashbacks, which begin with the third paragraph and constitute most of the narration. Quickly, I am drawn into this account of Be's journey with her mother from their clan's home in the north to live with Be's grandfather, who works for a white owner of a remote farm, called Ontevrede, in the Gobabis district.

During the years that Be and her mother live at Ontevrede, Be matures from a young child to an adolescent, slowly losing her childhood innocence as she discovers secrets about the boss and his deeply troubled wife, who befriends and educates Be, and about her own mother, Aia. When Be learns these things, she becomes deeply disillusioned—a classic coming-of-age *theme*, when realization of parental faults dashes childhood images of perfection. That theme relates to a National Council for the Social Studies (NCSS) curriculum standard under "Individual Development and Identity" (NCSS, n.d., Thematic Strands, para. 14) of personal identity development in the context of family, community, and society. Be, like other young people, must find her own separate identity and accept the adult world of humans—even parents—with frailties.

Another clear *theme* in this novel is the clash between indigenous cultures and dominant outside colonizers whose modernity threatens a traditional way of life. The current lives of people like the Bushmen have become degraded by removal from their land to "locations" established by white settlers, lack of meaningful employment, and alcohol abuse. Be learns this from her grandfather in answer to her question about why he chose to stay at Ontevrede, rather than return to his people, and it is symbolized by Be's song, which appears at the beginning and end of the story: "The smoke in the flames of the fires of Bushmanland . . . and the soft gray dust—before our footsteps were blown out." This image could be seen as reflecting the common misperception by outsiders, as expressed by Min, the white boss's wife, when she tells Be, "You come from . . . a proud, dying race. There are hardly any of you left" (p. 23). Min's assertion contrasts with Be's knowledge that, far from becoming extinct (like a prehistoric creature), her people were reproducing abundantly. Later, Be informs a reporter who visits the farm and inquires if she is "a real, live Bushman" that "I am a Ju/'hoan of Eastern Bushmanland and I am also real" (p. 35). Thus, although the former way of life, in a sense, is dying and must change, we later learn that some Bushmen were actively involved in the independence movement and reinventing their place in the new country. This concept matches the NCSS curricular theme that "cultures are dynamic and ever-changing" (NCSS, n.d., Thematic Strands, para. 6).

In the story's conclusion, Be is literally coaxed back to life by Khu, a political activist for her people, who tells her, "It's no use trying to go back . . . to an old life that doesn't—that can't—exist anymore" (p. 92). But, "what times there are ahead for us! The best of times . . . . For too long now we have been speaking as people who do not believe in themselves. . . . You can't die. Not now, when everything is beginning" (pp. 92–93). Khu asks her to join him in creating a new, inclusive nation. This *theme* of involvement in the political process and developing a sense of personal agency complements the NCSS curricular strand, "Civic Ideals and Practices" (NCSS, n.d., Thematic Strands, para. 33), and specifically responds to the questions for students: "What is the role of the citizen? . . . How can I make a positive difference?" (para. 34). In becoming involved in the process, young people also must recognize "the relationships between ideals and practice," (para. 34) another NCSS concept. Be faces a decision between killing herself after her ideals are dashed and living to work for a better, realistic future for her people.

Be's *character* develops believably and consistently, as portrayed through her memories and actions, from a naïve young child to a questioning, independent adolescent who learns many unsettling secrets. Appropriately, the story, narrated from her *point of view,* shows us her inner thoughts and feelings, and readers know only as much as Be did at the time about which she is remembering. *Stylistically,* the use of extended flashbacks complements the point of view, making the narrative sound like Be is reflecting upon the events at a later time. In addition, many instances of foreshadowing keep readers in suspense but also anticipating future events. Thus, the *plot,* with these elements and its unusual beginning, is highly original and immediately captures the reader's attention. The flashbacks and foreshadowing also tie all events together into a well-constructed narrative. As a critical reader, I judge that this book measures well by literary criteria for good literature.

Song of Be (Beake, 1995) also resonates strongly with another book I might use in my social studies classes when we study the native peoples of North America: *Julie of the Wolves,* by Jean Craighead George (1972). This classic novel also depicts the clash between a traditional way of life and modern civilization for a young Alaska native, as symbolized by her very name, Miyax/Julie. Her culture, like many other Native American cultures, has been degraded by Western civilization in similar ways that the Bushmen have suffered. In addition, Miyax is disillusioned when she discovers that her idealized father is deeply implicated in the changes she so resists. The more I contemplate them, the more remarkably parallel and intriguing the themes of these two books seem to me. I also consider how pairing the novels in my class might help my students not only to learn about a different culture within our own country but also provide a helpful context for learning about a culture from a place (Namibia) that might seem very remote to them—another connection with the NCSS strand of "Culture" for understanding multiple perspectives of "people in our nation and throughout the world" (NCSS, n.d., Thematic Strands, para. 5). We could have a rich study comparing not only the cultures but also the two protagonists and their experiences, thoughts, and feelings. *Julie of the Wolves* also has literary acclaim, as the winner of the Newbery Medal, so I am confident of these two books' literary merit.

However, how authentic are these books? I learn from Lesley Beake's website (www.lesleybeake.co.za/) about her work with an anthropologist, begun prior to Namibian independence, as founders of the Village Schools Project in Nyae Nyae, Namibia, the setting for *Song of Be* (Beake, 1995). Recently, she initiated a new project with the people of Nyae Nyae to develop a website (www.kalaharipeoples.net/) to provide a virtual space for networking and exchange of information among contemporary Kalahari communities and individuals throughout Southern Africa. On it, the San and other indigenous Kalahari dwellers speak in their own voices to each other and to interested people outside their communities. (Kalahari Peoples Network, 2010, para. 8)

On this website, I learn more about Be's people, and a page on the site, called "Primary School," includes information particularly addressed to students. From all this searching, I see that Beake is a knowledgeable outsider dedicated to the culture of which she writes.

Jean Craighead George's website (www.jeancraigheadgeorge.com/) tells me about her background in a family of naturalists; her dual science-literature bachelor's degree; her summer at the Naval Arctic Research Laboratory in Barrow, Alaska, among wolf researchers; her two sequels to this book; and the nearly one hundred books she has written, virtually all on environmental and nature topics. I am impressed with her credentials, and I believe both authors have credible expertise about the subjects of their books.

Still, I realize that both women are white and not deep insiders of the cultures about which they write in these books. Both have been questioned about their status and authority to write about the cultures. George has been criticized for inaccuracies and stereotypes in her portrayal of the Iñupiat culture (see Martha Stackhouse's, 2006, review of the book on the Alaska Native Knowledge Network website ankn.uaf.edu/IKS/HAIL/JulieWolves.html, for example) or presenting it as becoming extinct (similar to the perception about Bushmen). Both authors have defended the terminology they call the people. In *Julie's Wolf Pack*, George (1997) explains why she refers to Miyax's people as "Eskimos," a term sometimes viewed as inaccurate or demeaning. In an author's note, she writes, "Currently the name *Eskimo* is being replaced by *Inuit* to identify the circumpolar Eskimo people living in North America, Greenland, and Siberia." However, "the native people of Alaska's North Slope call themselves Eskimos or Iñupiat Eskimos." Likewise, Beake (1995) defends her use of "Bushmen," explaining in her author's note, "Much has been written about [the Ju/'hoan] people, who are sometimes called the San, but who prefer to be known as the Bushmen." At least both authors acknowledge the controversy and explain their rationales for the language they use, citing the native people's own preferences.

Another way of dealing with authenticity, besides examining the author's credentials, is to accept the reader's responsibility, as literary scholar Daniel Hade (1997) states, to read multiculturally. (Also, in the context of multicultural children's literature, Botelho and Rudman, 2009, call this type of reading "critical multicultural analysis.") Here, we adapt the concept for our purposes as responsibility to read *globally*. In fact, this is signified by our book title, and we address reading globally throughout this text in two senses. The first meaning, as noted earlier in this chapter, is to read *widely* and in literature from and about lands beyond our national borders. The second sense, being specifically discussed here, is to read *critically* and with all the techniques described in this chapter in terms of authenticity and literary merit. Thus, authors alone do not bear all the responsibility for these two broad aspects; readers must educate themselves to be thoughtfully critical in responses to books—especially when those books are outside our own realm of experience and knowledge. Instead of simply rejecting any book that seems problematic in any way, we should teach our students to do this kind of reading, also. In the long run, we will be teaching them more than we would by avoiding all controversies. Furthermore, this kind of reading conforms with national standards for both English language arts and social studies to obtain information from a variety of sources and analyze its reliability in terms of accuracy and credibility and to read critically by identifying the author's purpose and perspective (National Council of Teachers of English, 1996). Having met these goals, I can confidently make an informed decision about whether these two books will be good additions to my teaching.

Evaluating Translated Books

If an international book is written in a language other than English, it will require translation. Thus, for translated books, an additional criterion for evaluating literary merit is the quality of the translation. By way of background to this issue, it's helpful to know a bit about the translation process. For one thing, good translation is not just a matter of literally changing words from one language into another or a simple linguistic exercise. A literal translation usually will sound stilted or clumsy—in short, poorly written. Expert translators, such as Anthea Bell or Cathy Hirano, consider the book's child audience, the translation's target culture, and the subtleties of both languages with which they are working. An additional complication may arise when the translator is not working with the original text's language, but from another translation. Finally, some genres are harder to translate than others. As noted by Freeman and Lehman (2001),

Nonfiction is . . . easier to translate than fiction because it deals with factual material that usually has more readily accessible language equivalents. Poetry, on the other hand, is . . . the most difficult because of the specific language patterns, rhythm, and rhyme. (p. 31)

The best translators work creatively to capture the author's spirit and convey that to the translation's intended audience, so they can understand and appreciate the text. Frequently, this requires some adaptation, but how much is necessary or appropriate is a fine line. After all, part of our goal is to expose American children to more international literature, but if translation removes too much cultural context, readers may not even be aware that they are reading an international book, which actually defeats its purpose! Even seemingly innocuous changes like Americanization of names or spelling—altered to ensure their marketability in the United States—can undermine the fundamental goal of broadening our students' literary and cultural experience. In the article "'This is NOT What I Wrote!': The Americanization of British Children's Books—Part I," Jane Whitehead (1996) points out that "titles, setting, character names, and culturally specific allusions may all be changed in addition to spelling, punctuation, vocabulary, and idiom" (p. 688). For instance, even the international best-selling Harry Potter books underwent some change in the United States. The title of the first book was changed from *Harry Potter and the Philosopher's Stone* (Rowling, 1997) to *Harry Potter and the Sorcerer's Stone* (Rowling, 1998) for publication in the United States. Tomlinson (1998) hopes that in editing an international book for the United States, "a balance is achieved between the book's integrity and its marketability so that the flavor of the book's origins is apparent, and yet the story is easily understood by the new audience" (p. 19).

What, then, are factors we should consider for good translation? Without violating the original work's integrity, a good translation should not sound translated, yet it should still make readers aware that they are *not* reading a book that was first published in English in the United States. It does mean that the translator should make sound decisions about preserving the original work's cultural context while also being sensitive to the intended audience. This involves considering how much background knowledge readers (especially young ones with less life experience) who may be unfamiliar with historical, political, geographical, or religious references will need. Literary references, everyday objects, customs, and activities often are culturally specific and will need to be explained. Humor also is frequently unique to a culture and, thus, requires explanation (which probably will ruin it), elimination, or translation with some cultural equivalent that the intended audience understands. Sometimes, there is a conflict of values, whereby a joke, practice, language, or graphic depiction (of violence or sex, for example) that is acceptable in the original culture seems offensive or too disturbing in the target culture. Tomlinson (1998) points out that publishers "must sometimes consider potential for censorship of international children's books in this country" (p. 18). Children's books from other countries generally deal with the content of sexuality and religion and with illustrations showing nudity in a more direct way than do books first published in the United States. (See Chapter 8 for further discussion of this issue.) Therefore, a translator may need to consider how to handle this sensitive content and yet remain faithful to the meaning of the text.

Language itself—its grammar, stylistic patterns, vocabulary, dialect, idioms, and word play—presents special challenges for translation. These aspects, in particular, can easily contribute to the text's reading difficulty for young readers. Finally, illustrations (while not typically considered in this context and certainly not the responsibility of the translator) are also subject to "translation," in a way. As noted in Chapter 6, unfamiliar illustration styles may present difficulties for a young American audience, a situation that can be dealt with two ways: The publisher of the translated work decides to alter or even replace the original illustrations with a more culturally accessible style, or we can educate our students' taste. We prefer the latter, which is the reason for reading globally.

| Figure 7.3 | Profile: Mitsumasa Anno |

Mitsumasa Anno is a prolific Japanese author and illustrator whose works combine art and mathematics in creative ways that invite further examination by his audience. Some of his books explore mathematical themes and puzzles, while others focus on his journeys, paying particular attention to similarities among humans around the world. Anno has received many awards over his career, but his international recognition soared when he won IBBY's Hans Christian Andersen Award for Illustration in 1984.

Anno was born in Tsuwano, Japan, in 1926. As a small child, he dreamed of being an artist. After fulfilling his draft requirements for the Japanese Army in World War II, Anno studied at the Yamaguchi Teacher Training College. Upon completion of his degree program in 1948, he became a teacher at a Tokyo elementary school.

In 1952, he married Midori Suetsugu, and they had a son, Masaichiro, and a daughter, Seiko. Anno continued to think about his boyhood dream of becoming an artist, and, after 10 years of teaching elementary school, he decided to resign from his teaching position. Upon his resignation, Anno began his career in art and book design, in which he continued to teach about the mysteries of mathematics, art, and the world. He published his first children's book, *Topsy-Turvies: Pictures to Stretch the Imagination* (1971), in Japan in 1968.

Anno's books fall into two thematic categories: mathematics and patterns, and journeys. In his mathematical and pattern books, Anno helps the reader explore complex mathematical concepts, such as fractals, and interesting patterns through both text and illustrations. Examples of this category are *Anno's Alphabet: An Adventure in Imagination* (1975) and *Anno's Magic Seeds* (1995). In his journey books, Anno reveals to readers how he sees a particular location, which includes not only what he actually sees but also pieces of local history, fiction, and art. Anno's journey books include *Anno's Journey* (1997) and *Anno's Spain* (2004). Anno's unique writing style, coupled with the intricate details of his illustrations, encourages readers to explore patterns, nature, and their own imaginations.

Anno's artistic style is a blend of Asian and European aesthetics using pen and ink, watercolor, collage, and woodcuts. Some of his earlier works, such as *Topsy-Turvies* (1971) and *Upside-Downers: More Pictures to Stretch the Imagination* (1971), show the influence of M. C. Escher. Other European artistic influences can be found throughout his books. In *Anno's Spain* (2004), for example, Anno includes a drawing of dripping clocks on one of the pages, a reference to the art of Salvador Dali.

Mitsumasa Anno resides in Japan with his family, but he enjoys traveling the world. He never leaves home without his sketchbook. His instincts guide him to the locations he wants to sketch, and he relies very little on photographs. Anno's work continues to be honored in his hometown of Tsuwano, where visitors can see nearly 2,700 exhibits of his work at the Anno Museum of Art.

—*Christina D. Bragg*

Conclusion

This chapter addresses selection and evaluation of global books. Table 7 summarizes the two broad areas—authenticity and literary quality—and the specific factors within those areas. We hope the checklist will be a helpful, handy guide while reading globally for making thoughtful, informed book selections. (Teachers also may consider using this guide in discussions with students to help them examine the merits of books read in class.) We will benefit if we take the risk of climbing that border fence and viewing the "whole wide world," as in Woodson's (2001) *The Other Side*, and sharing what we see with our students.

Table 7   Questions for Evaluating Global Books

EVALUATING AUTHENTICITY
Author's Background
What is the author's status relative to the culture being depicted (i.e., clear insider, some inside knowledge/experience, marginal, relies on research only)?
Other Qualifications: Is the author widely traveled?   Does the author have clear expertise on the topic?   Has the author received literary recognition for this or other books?
Author's Attitude Toward the Book's Topic: Is the author respectful of the culture?   Is the author sympathetic toward the characters?   Does the author show clear understanding of the characters' experiences?   Does the author treat the subject matter as strange, exotic, or foreign to readers' experiences?   Does the author sound condescending?
Accuracy
Does the book seem accurate (based upon my knowledge, experience, or research)?   Is additional information provided by the author (i.e., in an author's note, about consultants for the book, or regarding references and resources consulted)?
Stereotyping
Are character stereotypes avoided?   Do relationships between characters avoid stereotypes of racial, ethnic, and class dominance?   Do the depictions of attitudes, values, and practices lead to stereotyping or fit previous stereotypes?   Are the settings depicted stereotypical of outsiders' preconceived ideas?   Are the illustrations free from stereotypes?
Readers' Perspective
Do readers from within the culture depicted view this book positively?   Would I feel positive if similar depictions were made about my own culture?
EVALUATING LITERARY MERIT
Fiction
Plot: Is the plot original and interesting?   Is the plot credible?   Is the plot well constructed?

Setting:

Is there an identifiable setting?

Does the setting seem authentic?

Themes:

Are there worthwhile themes?

Do the themes emerge naturally from the story?

Does the author avoid didacticism?

Characters:

Are the characters believable and consistent?

Are the characters well developed?

Style:

Is the writing style engaging?

Is the writing style appropriate for the tone of the story?

Does the style complement other literary elements of the story?

Point of View:

Is the point of view appropriate to the story?

Illustrations:

Are the illustrations high quality?

Are the illustrations appropriate for the story?

Do the illustrations contribute to the story?

Overall Design:

Is the book well-designed?

Is the design appropriate for the story?

Nonfiction

Is the content accurate?

Is there adequate coverage of the topic?

Is the author objective, or does the author have a particular perspective?

Is the author's perspective clearly acknowledged?

Is the book well organized?

Is the book written clearly?

Is the book's format appropriate?

Translation

Does the translation seem to preserve the integrity of the original work (including names)?

Does the author provide enough background information for the reader?

Do the language and writing sound natural?

Is the humor understandable and appropriate?

Are there problematic aspects with the book's content in my cultural context?

Are the illustrations the original ones for the book?

8

Frequently Asked Questions About Global Children's Literature

In our work with classroom teachers, we have noted the questions they often ask as they focus on increasing their use of global children's literature. Reading this book is certainly a great start, and we hope that the books we discuss in each chapter will help with decisions about purchases and curriculum. Two things are important to remember—first, increasing your use of global children's literature can be done gradually and doesn't have to be accomplished overnight. The important thing is to be intentional, looking for global literature and always thinking about how it might contribute to your daily lessons. Next, remember that support for this goal can increase as you work with your fellow educators to make the use of global literature not only a classroom goal but also a building and district goal. We hope that the questions and answers below help you to reach your goals for students' learning experiences with global children's literature and for enlisting support for these goals.

1. How can I fund the purchase of global children's literature for my classroom and school library?

You could start by reviewing your own collection and working with your fellow teachers to do the same. You may be surprised to find global literature that you already have! Look closely at information about the author and illustrator and examine the content to see if the book fits with our definition—books about or from other countries (published initially either in the United States or abroad) that are available in the United States. The next step is to enlist the help of your school librarian to identify global literature that is already in the school's collection. Depending on your needs, your librarian may be able to either compile a list of specific groups of books to provide easy access when you need them or even place those collections in a special part of your library so that teachers can access them easily when needed. These collections could be author studies like the books by South African author Niki Daly, a single genre like global poetry, or a collection of books about a particular part of the world like South Africa. None of these suggestions require additional funds; rather, they can happen when you approach the books that you already have with the intent to locate global literature.

Your parent-teacher organization might be another source for books. Perhaps the group would agree to buy a collection of global folktales one year and books by favorite authors the next. You might also approach your local service club to request funds. For example, Rotary International has a global perspective and might fund a collection of books for your school. You could also look for local and state grants from philanthropic organizations. Many require just a few pages of explanation rather than a lengthy application. You can lean on the chapters in this book to justify your request and explain the importance of students having access to global literature.

Another idea is to create a Birthday Book Club for which students can select a new book from a collection and donate the funds for that book rather than bringing snacks to celebrate their special day. You could read this book to the class as a special birthday treat and put a book plate inside honoring the student's birthday and donation. Perhaps the library would agree to keep the cost of the book low, maybe $8 to $10, to encourage greater participation.

2. How should we decide which books to buy?

This review of books you already have as suggested above is important for the next step—identifying the holes in your collection. Do you need more books by a particular author, of a certain genre, or on a topic to meet the learning goals of your students and curriculum? Once you answer those questions, you can work with your school leadership or literacy team to see if a portion of your school library budget could be dedicated to global literature each year. Perhaps several colleagues might be willing to help you prioritize the books that are most important to add to the collection each year. The titles in this book can be a start for your list as well as the websites suggested in various chapters. Professional journals focusing on children's literature more broadly, such as *The Horn Book, Journal of Children's Literature, Language Arts,* or *The Reading Teacher,* provide reviews of books in every issue that can be scanned as you look for global literature titles. Or, publications like *Bookbird: A Journal of International Children's Literature* review books that are specifically global. You will also find the information about USBBY's Outstanding International Books in Resource B (on the companion CD) to be helpful.

3. How can I work with colleagues to plan for using global children's literature across the grades?

Working with fellow teachers and media staff to identify global literature that you already possess and needed titles to add to your collection as suggested in FAQ 1 is an excellent way to begin planning with your colleagues. This search will raise the level of the group members' awareness about the importance of global literature and also their familiarity with books already in the school. You might want to initiate a teachers' book club to select a set of books to read and then discuss either during lunch or online through an instant message chat, e-mail, or communication tools available at your school website. Your students may also want to get involved as they read global literature and post their reviews online! Books with a wide audience could be quickly introduced at a staff meeting or in a weekly staff e-mail with a scan of the book cover. The book could also be displayed prominently in the school media center or library as the Global Book of the Week to encourage teachers and students to read it. These activities may lead to a more formal book club facilitated by a local children's literature professor who may also be able to provide university credit for the group's study.

These efforts will then support your grade-level work as you meet with colleagues to plan specific units of study based upon local, state, and national standards. The content-area chapters of this book offer many ideas about books that meet standards. Specific teaching and learning activities could be designed to benefit all teachers in your grade as they implement the curriculum. Some schools schedule art, music, and physical education classes so that teachers can plan together, but be sure to also share your plans with teachers of special classes to request their ideas about ways that your students' work in art, music, and physical education can connect with their regular classroom study. The books and ideas in Chapter 6 will be particularly helpful as you work with art and music teachers. The physical education teacher may also have ideas about ways that global dances, movements, and games can connect with your areas of study.

4. What's the best way to handle sensitive topics like war, prejudice, human injustices, and cultural taboos like bodily functions or practices?

This question provides a great topic for your book study group to explore. One of the first things to ask is, Who should read or listen to this book? Some may assume that picture books are for younger readers and chapter books are for older students, but you'll need to dig deeper into each book to really answer this question. For example, *Rose Blanche*, by Christophe Gallaz, (1985) and illustrated by 2008 Hans Christian Andersen Award-winner Roberto Innocenti, may seem at first to be a simple picture book about a young girl and her curiosity about where a boy is taken by soldiers in Nazi Germany. Looking closely, however, readers will see that the book's content brings the horrors of World War II to life through Rose Blanche's discovery of starving inmates of a concentration camp. Clearly, this book demands a more mature audience. One member of your group may volunteer to share a particular book on a sensitive topic with students and then report back to the group about the students' responses and questions, which will help the group think through matching books to readers. You may be tempted to avoid all controversy, but denying the complexities of our world and more sensitive issues, like war, does not help students develop a global perspective. The key is to thoughtfully present books developmentally suitable for your students and discuss them with respect. Books like *Rose Blanche* are important opportunities to help students understand historical events by allowing them to step into her life for a moment. These understandings are much less likely to come from content in a social studies textbook.

Sexual orientation may also be a delicate topic in some schools. Jamie Naidoo (2009) surveyed librarians in public libraries and documented evidence of bias against books about children with same sex parents, ranging from totally excluding such books from their collections to limiting the books to the parent section, as the titles would be "too sensitive" for the children's department. Consider, for example, Linda de Haan and Stern Nijland's (2000, 2004) *King & King* and its sequel, *King & King & Family*, which focus on a young prince who falls in love with another prince. They marry, and the two adopt a little girl to make their family complete. Originally published in The Netherlands, these two picture books take a matter-of-fact stance toward the marriage of the two princes as well as their daughter's adoption. A Kirkus review on the back cover noted that *King & King* "firmly challenges the assumptions established and perpetuated by the entire canon of children's picture books."

What if a parent objects to a book? This question deserves serious attention and the development of a clear censorship policy at the district and school levels so that everyone knows the process if a book is challenged. Having a written policy helps to diffuse some of the emotion that often accompanies these requests. Help for designing your policy can easily be found on the Web. The National Council of Teachers of English (www.ncte.org) and the International Reading Association (www.reading .org) have guidelines, articles, position statements, and other resources on their websites for thinking about censorship and designing a local policy. Two excellent articles by Megan Schliesman and Christine A. Jenkins, both in the January 2008 issue of *Language Arts*, include resources for educators about censorship. *Shattering the Looking Glass: Challenge, Risk & Controversy in Children's Literature*, edited by Susan S. Lehr (2008), includes chapters on censorship, politics, ethnicity, and sexual orientation. Additional information can be found in texts like *Charlotte Huck's Children's Literature*, by Barbara Kiefer (2010), or by visiting the website of the American Library Association (www.ala.org).

5. How should I respond if parents object to a book?

If your school already has a policy about censorship, your first response will be to give the written policy to the parent and initiate the process without confrontation. In some policies, the parent must first read the book before making a judgment to assure that the objection is not based on limited information, such as the title of the book, or hearsay, such as another person's opinion. Then, ask the parent to put the objection in writing, and explain that you will also write your rationale for selecting the book. You might also add reviews of the book from professional journals and other awards or recognitions that the book may have received. Then, approach your principal for guidance as to the next step, which might be convening a review committee composed of parents, teachers, media staff, and administrators to study the written arguments and consider the request. Parents need assurance that their objections are being heard. In fact, this situation may be an opportunity for parents to learn more about the curriculum and characteristics of quality books. In this sensitive situation, avoid emotional responses, and keep the details of the conversations at a professional level to ensure appropriate consideration of the request.

6. How can I help my students relate to places, people, times, and events they have never seen, heard, or experienced?

We hope you noticed that some of the books we discussed in each chapter are linked to books that students may already know and commonly read in U.S. classrooms. Such connections can bridge the gap between the known and unknown. Linking a more familiar version of the Cinderella story with one from another part of the world supports understanding. Another idea is to use the Internet, videos, DVDs, and other nonprint materials. Viewing a movie about South Africa is an opportunity to learn about the country and its people, which supports comprehension while reading or listening to books from or about South Africa. You might also send a brief survey to parents through an e-mail or in hard copy asking if they have pictures from international travels or know someone from another country. This could provide a wealth of opportunities for guest speakers, slide shows, and exhibits of art, clothing, or other artifacts from a particular part of the world. These experiences can support students' research about countries in the area of the world you are studying. Finally, taking time to study the books' illustrations is another way to learn more about a place or culture. Select special places in the book to stop and discuss what students can learn about the characters, setting, or plot from studying the photographs or illustrations. This will contribute to your students' visual literacy as they realize the importance of "reading" the illustrations, too!

7. How can I help parents understand the importance of global literature?

The students in your class can be very helpful in educating their parents. As you discuss your goals with your students and identify global literature you share with them, be sure to have them tell their parents about it, too. In the younger grades, you could remind them of a message to tell their parents as they line up to go home. You could also create a shared writing each week about the books you are reading that you copy and send home or e-mail to parents. This would certainly help when parents ask, "What did you do in school today?" The student would have an answer all ready to go! Older students might create daily logs of their reading with the intent of taking them home regularly to inform their parents about the books they are reading or listening to. If your school has a newsletter, a brief article about the global literature you've been studying will heighten parents' awareness of the importance of thinking, studying, and reading globally. As more teachers in your building begin to use global literature, you might also create a worldwide fair to showcase students' work and provide a time to share the dances, drawings, responses, writings, and projects students have done as they read books from an international perspective. Perhaps your local parent-teacher organization might sponsor a visit from an author or illustrator whose books are global that would include time for parents to come and learn more about the writer's craft or artist's techniques. (See also the ideas in FAQ 1 about parents.)

8. How do I fit global literature into our district-mandated curricula that occupy much of the day?

Global literature should not be an "add-on" to the daily schedule. The key to this question is integration, starting with linking language arts to all other content areas. Reading books about a content-area subject like social studies accomplishes dual goals—students increase their reading abilities while reading appropriate books about a topic and learn more about the topic as well. Having a wide range of interesting books available about a particular topic will support deeper understanding than relying solely on a textbook, and it will also meet a range of reading abilities. Allington (2009) argues that learning for struggling readers increases if they have books that they can read successfully.

Because textbooks target a particular grade level, such texts may be difficult for readers who struggle. Collections of interesting books, however, help teachers match books to readers. Allington supports this claim by citing a meta-analysis of 22 studies by Guthrie and Humenick that documented much higher comprehension achievement when students had ready access to interesting texts (p. 71).

Writing is also an easy integration. You can study many genres of writing through content-area books and writing assignments—how to compare and contrast, design and describe an experiment, take notes as data, write a biography, or compose a convincing argument based on facts. Integrating with literacy takes much less class time than separating each subject area.

Integration across content areas with thematic studies is also a way to accomplish several goals at the same time (as described in Chapter 2). Link historical events with scientific knowledge available at that time. Or work with music and art teachers to encourage them to use the books offered in Chapter 6. And of course, science lessons also have great potential for integrating with math.

The ideas in FAQs 1 and 2 above will also help you to integrate content areas. At grade-level meetings, discuss global books for content areas, and make sure they are readily available when you need them. At the district level, join a committee working on a list of relevant books for various topics that support student learning goals from the curriculum. These lists can be shared across the district to inform purchasing decisions.

9. How does global literature contribute to meeting state and national standards?

We purposely highlighted national standards in the chapters about individual content areas to illustrate how global children's literature supports each area. If you look back at those chapters, you'll find that national standards are typically more general than specific and are more likely to encourage integration than a focus on a single skill. Both of these qualities are opportunities for global children's literature in the classroom. In fact, there are specific standards in language arts, social studies, and STEM education that specifically require a global perspective, which the books suggested in those chapters are clearly needed to accomplish. We propose that global literature is not an "extra if we have time"; rather, it is an essential element to achieve state and national standards.

10. Will using global literature raise test scores?

To answer this question, we need to step back and consider what we know about learning. First, learners need to be engaged. We believe that global children's literature provides meaningful reading experiences for children that are interesting and deepen understandings. Quality books heighten engagement, and learners need that to be successful. If the textbook is the center of learning experiences, many children will be unable to successfully read and understand important concepts. Having books of varied difficulty ensures that every child will be able to read successfully and share new learning from that particular book. We believe that learning happens when the learner is motivated and willing to learn independently. Students who spend the most time reading and writing both in and out of school tend to learn more across the year. Global literature can motivate students to read fascinating stories in school and spend time with more books at home. Finally, we believe that what the teacher values, students will value. A teacher who is excited about books, provides many learning opportunities with books, and shares excitement with the class will support their learning in important ways.

9

What's Next?
Going Global and
Bringing It Home

We started this book with Miss Rumphius, in the Barbara Cooney (1982) title by that name, who traveled to faraway places and returned to make her home by the sea more beautiful. Like her, you too can go global through children's literature, and you too can make your part of the world more beautiful by bringing the global home for your students. In this last chapter, we address how you can launch this exciting journey and offer final words of support.

Getting Started

If you have gotten this far, then you have a good start because you have read this book! That in itself shows interest in and commitment to infusing a global perspective through your teaching. And if you have read this book, we hope that you are convinced about our key points.

First, we addressed the importance of global literature for connecting children to the world and how these books can meet children's cognitive, emotional, moral, and social development in an increasingly diverse country within today's expanding international context. Statistics for population trends, current events around the world, and economic globalization provide strong evidence for these national and global realities.

Second, we stated our goals for global literature: building bridges of international understanding through books that accurately reflect children in all their diversity *and* that open onto the lives of other children with different experiences. We embedded these goals within a literary framework that integrates theme studies throughout the curriculum. In every case, we also related our ideas to national curriculum content standards to demonstrate how these can be addressed.

Third, we discussed how to find, select, and evaluate global literature. Because we have intensively researched and taught books with an international focus for more than a decade, we well understand the difficulties of locating this literature. Add to that the challenges of determining the authenticity and quality of books we do find, and it becomes clear that teaching with global literature is often harder work than using more familiar books. We firmly believe, however, that the extra effort will afford us and our students much greater satisfaction and will achieve far better the goals described above.

Fourth, in addition to the issue of selection and evaluation of global literature, we considered other concerns that we often hear teachers express, such as purchasing books with tight budgets, collaborating with colleagues, handling sensitive topics and possible parental objections, convincing parents and others of the importance of global literature, making global literature relevant to students we teach, fitting global literature into the curriculum, and recognizing how such literature can contribute to meeting curriculum standards and enhancing student achievement. These are all legitimate points, and we have to offer reasonable, practical solutions. We know how dedicated teachers are and how many demands they face. All three of us are former classroom teachers, and we continue to work closely with teachers today. Because we care deeply about children's future and the world they will inherit, we are passionate about our topic and have tried to make it one that teachers will embrace as valuable. We hope that the vignettes and teaching ideas we have included help to illustrate some possibilities in actual classrooms.

Finally, to support teachers in their work, we also provided resources and advice for keeping up with global literature. We hope this book itself will be an important resource for teachers. The teaching suggestions we offer are not prescriptions but possibilities that we hope will stimulate your own ideas. In our view, one of the most helpful parts of this book is the companion CD, which you no doubt have already found and used, with the extensive An Annotated List of 341 Children's Books Cited in the Book. In addition to bibliographic information, we suggest interest levels for the books; the annotations provide brief book summaries and note their genres. Other useful resources for keeping up with global literature—such as websites, publications, and awards—are provided on the CD in Resource B, Resources for Locating and Learning More About Global Children's Literature. The profiled authors and illustrators also can be good starting points for learning about global literature. Once you begin to explore some of these resources, you will discover others that are informative, and soon you will acquire a wealth of possibilities.

Now that you have reached the end of this book, what can you do next? Some of the following points are addressed more extensively earlier, but we reiterate and consider them in slightly different ways here. First, as we suggested in Chapter 8, identify the global literature that already exists in your classroom collection or school library. Then, starting with these books, review your curriculum guidelines to find places where this literature can be inserted. In Chapters 3 through 6, we have shown how national standards can be met with global literature, but you should adapt these ideas to your own local curriculum. If you match literature with the curriculum, you will strengthen your rationale for teaching with global books. Next, as you align what books you currently have with curricular goals, you probably also will recognize where your available global titles are thin or lacking. Some of those areas—especially the ones that seem most associated with potential international topics—could benefit from the inclusion of more global literature. These are the places on which you should focus efforts to globalize your teaching. Finally, to do this, look for additional global books that would fit these topics. Check for suitable titles in resources cited on the companion CD in Resource B and in Resource C—An Annotated List of 341 Children's Books Cited in the Book.

Final Thoughts

By now, you are probably eager to embark on this journey; but before you leave the home port, we offer a few final thoughts of encouragement. We know how easily we can be overwhelmed when we start something new, and if we are not careful, being overwhelmed can cause us to retreat from the entire venture. Thus, we suggest that you list your goals, and don't hesitate to think big as you decide these goals. However, then you need to make a plan to reach your destination. Prioritize, and start with a few steps that are most achievable; don't try to accomplish everything at once. When you have attained these, you should celebrate, but move on! Keep challenging yourself with meeting all your goals and then setting new ones. Think of arriving at one destination on this journey as an invitation to move on before too long.

In addition, whenever we travel to new places (in the world or in our teaching), we can expect to experience culture shock—a feeling that may make us wish to give up and go home. This can be disorienting, so give yourself time to adjust, and don't journey alone, if possible. Develop a support system of fellow travelers—other teachers who share your goals. As suggested in Chapter 8, you might collaborate with colleagues in your school or district. You can find out where your travel plans overlap, work together in those areas, and encourage each other to continue the journey.

However, the more you read global children's books and expand your horizons, the more familiar they become, and the less intimidating it will be to teach with this literature. We also urge you to continue globalizing your worldview by sampling the adult titles we have suggested in Resource A, Further Recommended Reading for Teachers, on the companion CD. One of the best organizations to both support and stimulate you professionally regarding global literature is the United States Board on Books for Young People (USBBY, www.usbby.org), a group of educators, librarians, authors, illustrators, publishers, and others dedicated to international literature. You can join USBBY, get involved, and meet enthusiastic, adventurous traveling companions. The IBBY regional conference, sponsored by USBBY every odd-numbered year, is an inspirational, global gathering held right here in the United States, where you can hear international children's writers, illustrators, and other speakers who will share perspectives from beyond our national borders.

We invite you to set out on this journey into our amazing, wide world with your students. Read globally, and your lives will all be better for it. As they say in South Africa, "Go well," or in France, "Bon voyage!"

References

Allington, R. L. (2009). *What really matters in response to intervention: Research-based designs.* Boston: Pearson.

American Himalayan Foundation. (2006). *American Himalayan Foundation.* Retrieved June 14, 2010, from http://www.himalayan-foundation.org/.

Apnicommunity.com. (2010, May 6). *Meet author Mem Fox.* Retrieved June 29, 2010, from http://videos.apnicommunity.com/Video,Item,53610658.html.

Asia/Pacific Cultural Centre for UNESCO. (2010, January 29). *Winning work collections of NOMA concours for picture book illustrations 1978–2008.* Retrieved June 12, 2010, from http://www.accu.or.jp/noma/english/e_index.html.

Association for Library Service to Children. (2010). *Welcome to the Pura Belpré Award home page!* Retrieved June 12, 2010, from http://www.ala.org/ala/mgrps/divs/alsc/awardsgrants/bookmedia/belpremedal/index.cfm.

Bartholet, J., & Stone, D. (2009, January 26). A team of expatriates. *Newsweek, 153,* 52–53.

Batchelder, M. L. (1966). Learning about children's books in translation. *ALA Bulletin, 60,* 33–42.

Benedict, S. (Ed.). (1992). *Beyond words: Picture books for older readers and writers.* Portsmouth, NH: Heinemann.

Bennet, M. (2007, June 4). "Tasting the Sky": An interview with Ibtisam Barakat. *The Nation.* Retrieved June 11, 2010, from http://www.thenation.com/doc/20070618/bennett/print.

Bishop, R. S. (Ed.). (1994). *Kaleidoscope: A multicultural booklist for grades K–8.* Urbana, IL: National Council of Teachers of English.

Botelho, M. J., & Rudman, M. K. (2009). *Critical multicultural analysis of children's literature: Mirrors, windows, and doors.* New York: Routledge.

Boughton, S. (2006). Shrinking world: Book fairs and the changing market. In D. Gebel (Ed.), *Crossing boundaries with children's books* (pp. 14–20). Lanham, MD: Scarecrow.

Cai, M. (2002). *Multicultural literature for children and young adults: Reflections on critical issues.* Westport, CT: Greenwood.

Center for Latin American and Caribbean Studies. (2007). *Américas book award for children's and young adult literature.* Retrieved June 12, 2010, from http://www4.uwm.edu/clacs/aa/index.cfm.

Clute, J., & Grant, J. (1997). *The encyclopedia of fantasy.* London: Orbit.

Delacre, L. (n.d.). *Lulu Delacre: Bilingual author and illustrator of children's books.* Retrieved July 1, 2010, from http://www.luludelacre.com/bio.htm.

Evans, C. S. (1987). Teaching a global perspective in elementary classrooms. *Elementary School Journal, 87,* 545–555.

Fountas, I. C., & Pinnell, G. S. (1996). *Guided reading: Good first teaching for all children.* Portsmouth, NH: Heinemann.

Fox, M. (2001). *Reading magic.* New York: Harcourt.

Freeman, E. B. (1999). Uri Orlev: International storyteller. *Journal of Children's Literature, 25*(1), 44–47.

Freeman, E. B., & Lehman, B. A. (2001). *Global perspectives in children's literature.* Boston: Allyn & Bacon.

Freeman, E. B., Lehman, B. A., & Scharer, P. L. (2007). The challenges and opportunities of international literature. In N. Hadaway & M. J. McKenna (Eds.), *Breaking boundaries with global literature: Celebrating diversity in K–12 classrooms* (pp. 33–51). Newark, DE: International Reading Association.

Frey, N., & Fisher, D. (2008). *Teaching visual literacy: Using comic books, graphic novels, anime, cartoons, and more to develop comprehension and thinking skills.* Thousand Oaks, CA: Corwin.

Friedman, T. (2007). *The world is flat: A brief history of the twenty-first century* (Further updated and expanded ed.). New York: Farrar, Straus and Giroux.

Garrett, J. (2003). IBBY's awards and selections: Can there be international standards of excellence? In L. Maissen (Ed.), *Proceedings of the 28th Congress of International Board on Books for Young People* (pp. 119–128). Basel, Switzerland: International Board on Books for Young People.

Garrett, J. (2008). Screams and smiles: On some possible human universals in children's book illustration. *Bookbird: A Journal of International Children's Literature, 46*(4), pp. 16–24.

Gebel, D. (Ed.). (2006). *Crossing boundaries with children's books.* Lanham, MD: Scarecrow.

Glistrup, E. (2002). *The Hans Christian Andersen Awards: 1956–2002.* Basel, Switzerland: International Board on Books for Young People.

Hadaway, N. L., & McKenna, M. J. (Eds.). (2007). *Breaking boundaries with global literature.* Newark, DE: International Reading Association.

Hade, D. D. (1997). Reading multiculturally. In V. J. Harris (Ed.), *Using multiethnic literature in the K–8 classroom* (pp. 233–256). Norwood, MA: Christopher-Gordon.

Hazard, P. (1944). *Books, children & men.* (M. Mitchell, Trans.). Boston: Horn Book.

International Children's Digital Library. (n.d.). *Our mission.* Retrieved June 29, 2010, from http://en.childrenslibrary.org/.

International Reading Association & National Council of Teachers of English. (1996). *Standards for the English language arts.* Newark, DE: International Reading Association; & Urbana, IL: National Council of Teachers of English.

Jane Addams Peace Association. (n.d.). *About the children's book awards.* Retrieved June 12, 2010, from http://www.janeaddamspeace.org/.

Jenkins, C. A. (2008). Book challenges, challenging books, and young readers: The research picture. *Language Arts, 85,* 228–236.

Jweid, R., & Rizzo, M. (2004). *Building character through multicultural literature: A guide for middle school readers.* Lanham, MD: Scarecrow.

Kalahari Peoples Network. (2010). *About the site.* Retrieved June 30, 2010, from http://www.kalaharipeoples.net/about.php.

Kids Can Press. (n.d.). *Katie Smith Milway, author.* Retrieved June 14, 2010, from http://www.kidscanpress.com/Canada/CreatorDetails.aspx?cid=200.

Kiefer, B. Z. (2010). *Charlotte Huck's children's literature* (10th ed.). New York: McGraw Hill.

Kohlberg, L. (1976). Moral stages and moralization: The cognitive-developmental approach. In T. Lickona (Ed.), *Moral development and behavior: Theory, research, and social issues* (pp. 31–53). New York: Holt.

Lauritzen, C., & Jaeger, M. (1997). *Integrating learning through story: The narrative curriculum.* Albany, NY: Delmar.

Lehman, B. A. (2006). Children's literature and national identity in the new South Africa. *Sankofa, 5,* 6–19.

Lehman, B. A. (2007). *Children's literature and learning: Literary study across the curriculum.* New York: Teachers College Press.

Lehman, B., & Crook, P. (1998). Doubletalk: A literary pairing of *The Giver* and *We Are All in the Dumps with Jack and Guy. Children's Literature in Education, 29,* 69–78.

Lehr, S. S. (Ed.). (2008). *Shattering the looking glass: Challenge, risk & controversy in children's literature.* Norwood, MA: Christopher-Gordon.

Lepman, J. (2002). *A bridge of children's books* (E. McCormick, Trans.). Dublin, Ireland: O'Brien. (Original work published 1964)

Milestones Project. (2010). *Mission & values.* Retrieved June 29, 2010, from http://milestonesproject.com/index.php/big_picture/mission_vision.

Miller, L. (2005, December 26). Far from Narnia: Philip Pullman's secular fantasy for children. *The New Yorker.* Retrieved June 11, 2010, from http://www.newyorker.com/archive/2005/12/26/051226fa_fact.

Morrison, J. S. (2006). *Attributes of STEM education.* Retrieved June 30, 2010, from http://www.tiesteach.org/documents/Jans%20pdf%20Attributes_of_STEM_Education-1.pdf.

Mortenson, G. (with Relin, D. O.). (2006). *Three cups of tea.* New York: Penguin.

Naidoo, J. C. (2009, July). *Focus on my family: An analysis of gay-themed picturebooks & public library services for LGBTQ children and children with same-sex parents.* Paper presented at the annual conference of the American Library Association, Chicago, IL.

National Council of the Social Studies. (n.d.). *Curriculum standards for social studies.* Retrieved June 14, 2010, from http://www.socialstudies.org/standards/introduction.

National Council of Teachers of English. (1996). *Standards for the English language arts.* Retrieved June 30, 2010, from http://www.ncte.org/library/NCTEFiles/Resources/Books/Sample/StandardsDoc.pdf.

Orlev, U. (1997). *The sandgame* (H. Halkin, Trans.). Kibbutz Dalia, Israel: Ghetto Fighters' House.

Orlev, U. (2005). *Poems from Bergen-Belsen, 1944.* Jerusalem, Israel: Yad Vashem.

Oxley, P. (1995). Literary tapestry: An integrated primary curriculum. In M. R. Sorensen & B. A. Lehman (Eds.), *Teaching with children's books: Paths to literature-based instruction* (pp. 213–217). Urbana, IL: National Council of Teachers of English.

Pappas, C. C., Kiefer, B. Z., & Levstik, L. S. (2006). *An integrated language perspective in the elementary school: An action approach* (4th ed.). Boston: Pearson/Allyn & Bacon.

Paterson, K. (2009, October 3). *Hans Christian Andersen authors speak out.* Talk given at the International Board on Books for Young People eighth annual conference, St. Charles, IL. Available from www.usbby.org.

Publishing Central. (2009, May 19). Bowker reports U.S. book production declines 3% in 2008, but "on demand" publishing more than doubles. *Publishing Central.* Retrieved June 11, 2010, from http://publishingcentral .com/blog/book-publishing/bowker-reports.

Pullman, P. (2005). Introduction. In J. Milton, *Paradise Lost* (pp. 1–10). Oxford, England: Oxford University Press.

Pullman, P. (2009). About Philip Pullman. In *Philip Pullman.* Retrieved June 11, 2010, from http://www.philip-pullman.com/about.asp.

Robb, L. (2003). *Teaching reading in social studies, science, and math.* New York: Scholastic.

Rochman, H. (1993). *Against borders: Promoting books for a multicultural world.* Chicago, IL: American Library Association.

Scharer, P. L. (2007). Talking about books to learn the writer's craft. In P. L. Scharer & G. S. Pinnell (Eds.), *Guiding K–3 writers to independence: The new essentials* (pp. 121–130). Columbus, OH: Literacy Collaborative at The Ohio State University.

Scharer, P. L., Freeman, E. B., Lehman, B. A., & Allen, V. G. (1993). Literacy and literature in elementary classrooms: Teachers' beliefs and practices. In D. J. Leu & C. K. Kinzer (Eds.), *Examining central issues in literacy research, theory, and practice* (pp. 359–366). Chicago: National Reading Conference 42nd Yearbook.

Scharioth, B. (2001). *The White Ravens.* Munich, Germany: International Youth Library.

Schliesman, M. (2008). Intellectual freedom. *Language Arts, 85,* 221–227.

Siu-Runyan, Y., & Faircloth, C. V. (Eds.). (1995). *Beyond separate subjects: Integrative learning at the middle level.* Norwood, MA: Christopher-Gordon.

Stackhouse, M. (2006, August 14). Honoring Alaska's indigenous literature [Review of the book *Julie of the wolves*]. Retrieved June 15, 2010, from ankn.uaf.edu/IKS/HAIL/JulieWolves.html.

Stan, S. (Ed.). (2002). *The world through children's books.* Lanham, MD: Scarecrow.

STEM Education Coalition. (n.d.). *STEM education coalition.* Retrieved June 14, 2010, from www.stemedcoalition.org.

Stirring the pot. (2009, January 26). *Newsweek, 153,* 70.

Strickland, T. (2009, January 28). *State of the state address.* Retrieved June 24, 2010, from http://www.governor.ohio.gov/GovernorsOffice/StateoftheState/ StateoftheState2009/tabid/984/Default.aspx.

Tiedt, I. M. (2000). *Teaching with picture books in the middle school.* Newark, DE: International Reading Association.

Tomlinson, C. (Ed.). (1998). *Children's books from other countries.* Lanham, MD: Scarecrow.

U.S. Census Bureau. (n.d.). *Fact sheet: U.S.A.* Retrieved June 24, 2010, from http://factfinder.census.gov/servlet/ACSSAFFFacts?_event=&geo_id= 01000US&_geoContext=01000US&_street=&_county=&_cityTown=&_

state=&_zip=&_lang=en&_sse=on&ActiveGeoDiv=&_useEV=&pctxt= fph&pgsl=010&_submenuId=factsheet_1&ds_name=DEC_2000_SAFF&_ ci_nbr=002&qr_name=DEC_2000_SAFF_R1010&reg=DEC_2000_SAFF_ R1010%3A002&_keyword=&_industry=.

Vardell, S. M. (2004). Children's books as best sellers: Their impact on the field of children's literature. *Journal of Children's Literature, 30*(1), 13–18.

Whitehead, J. (1996). "This is NOT what I wrote!": The Americanization of British children's books. *The Horn Book Magazine, 72,* 687–693.

World Health Organization. (2010). *Millennium development goals.* Retrieved June 24, 2010, from http://www.who.int/topics/millennium_ development_goals/en/.

Yenika-Agbaw, V. (2008). *Representing Africa in children's literature: Old and new ways of seeing.* New York: Routledge.

Zarnowski, M. (2003). *History makers: A questioning approach to reading & writing biographies.* Portsmouth, NH: Heinemann.

Zerbonia, R. G. (2010). Tololwa Mollel. *Answers.com.* Retrieved June 30, 2010, from http://www.answers.com/topic/tololwa-mollel.

Index

CORWIN

A SAGE Company

The Corwin logo—a raven striding across an open book—represents the union of courage and learning. Corwin is committed to improving education for all learners by publishing books and other professional development resources for those serving the field of PreK–12 education. By providing practical, hands-on materials, Corwin continues to carry out the promise of its motto: **"Helping Educators Do Their Work Better."**